ASPECTS OF THE WAY

ASPECTS OF THE WAY
BEING MEDITATIONS AND STUDIES
IN THE LIFE OF JESUS CHRIST

By

A. D. MARTIN

౿

CAMBRIDGE
AT THE UNIVERSITY PRESS
MCMXXIV

CAMBRIDGE
UNIVERSITY PRESS

University Printing House, Cambridge CB2 8BS, United Kingdom

Cambridge University Press is part of the University of Cambridge.

It furthers the University's mission by disseminating knowledge in the pursuit of
education, learning and research at the highest international levels of excellence.

www.cambridge.org
Information on this title: www.cambridge.org/9781107458741

© Cambridge University Press 1924

First published 1924
First paperback edition 2014

A catalogue record for this publication is available from the British Library

ISBN 978-1-107-45874-1 Paperback

I GIVE THIS BOOK
MOST GRATEFULLY
TO
MY WIFE

PREFACE

THE Founder of Christianity once described Himself as THE WAY. It would appear also that the Religion He founded was first so called by its disciples, and that the term CHRISTIANITY only arose out of the talk of the Pagan World about it. The Revisers of the Authorised Version of the New Testament have indicated for us this earliest designation of our Faith by the renderings given of Acts ix. 2, xix. 9, xix. 23, xxii. 4, xxiv. 22. Perhaps if the name had been preserved in common use the Church would have been delivered from some of its unprogressive moods. I have ventured to adopt it in the title of this book because my whole conception of religious institutions, scriptures and doctrines is that they are valueless unless they are instruments, methods, or spiritual plant for establishing the contact of the Soul with God.

Some of the chapters which follow have appeared before. *Elect Shepherds* was published as

a Christmas booklet in 1923 and the edition
exhausted. The chapter on the Temptation
appeared in the *Expository Times*, vol. xxxiv.
That on the Mind of Jesus was contributed
under the title of *The Seamless Robe* to *The
London Quarterly Review* (April, 1918). *The Cup*
was published in *The Interpreter* (April, 1915)
and *The Ascension* in *The Expositor* (November,
1918). For the last chapter I have drawn
largely upon an article *One Avenue to God*,
which I contributed to *The Hibbert Journal* in
April, 1914.

I thank the Editors and Publishers of these
Magazines for their kindness in permitting me
to use these materials from their pages. I have
availed myself of their courtesy more fully in
some cases than in others. In no instance am
I simply republishing. Each paper has been
revised. In some instances I have made a good
deal of alteration, always, I hope, in the direction of greater lucidity. I have also to thank
Mr Wilfrid Meynell for permission to quote in
full (on p. 169) the beautiful Advent Meditation
contained in the Poems of Alice Meynell.

My Scripture quotations are nearly always from the Revised Version.

I have avoided footnotes and references as much as possible, my object being to interest the general reader rather than to attract the theologian. If my pages should be perused by the latter I trust he will be able to detect the processes of my judgments where results only are stated.

A. D. M.

THE GROVE,
DANBURY,
ESSEX.

CONTENTS

PROLOGUE

ELECT SHEPHERDS

Secret was the garden;
Set i' the pathless awe
Where no star its breath can draw.
Life, that is its warden,
Sits behind the fosse of death. Mine eyes saw not, and
I saw.

FRANCIS THOMPSON.

Blazing logs threw a golden light upon the faces of the three or four shepherds who had charge of the Temple sheep pasturing near Bethlehem. No ordinary herdsmen were these men, who from afar served the altar of the Lord in Jerusalem. That they were devout is evident not only from their vocation but from their speech and their instant praise of God. Also in their hearts was the national hope.

Many a Hebrew in those days was looking for *the Consolation of Israel*. Many were searching the Scriptures of the prophets to see *what time or what manner of time the Spirit of Christ which was in them did point unto*. And the Temple shepherds, as they lay around their fire, talked of the one theme which was then talked of wherever the poor in spirit met together. One, it may be, had a scroll from the Book of Isaiah, and, turning its characters towards the firelight, read to his fellows,

The government shall be upon His shoulder: and His Name shall be called Wonderful, Counsellor, Mighty God, Everlasting Father, Prince of Peace.

And presently another played on his lute marriage music of the Messianic psalm men called *Shoshannim*, that is *Lilies*, for was it not a music liquid, and as gold set in white, like the canopied flowers of the field? As he played his fellows sang,

Thy throne, O God, is for ever and ever:
A sceptre of equity is the sceptre of Thy kingdom.
Thou hast loved righteousness, and hated wickedness:
Therefore God, Thy God, hath anointed Thee
With the oil of Gladness above Thy fellows.
All Thy garments smell of myrrh, and aloes, and cassia;
Out of ivory palaces stringed instruments have made Thee glad.

Now those who know how to climb the higher paths of prayer sometimes come upon that secret garden of the Lord, which is

Set i' the pathless awe.

They encounter the breath of the Infinite and

are conscious of a Spiritual Presence multitudinous and yet one. To such it will not appear
incredible that God should have granted to the
Elect Shepherds an experience never to be repeated, because never again to be enshrined
within the same stupendous circumstances. For
when Christ was born at Bethlehem the long
centuries of preparation reached their end, and
once again God made Man with as absolute
a new beginning as when, from earlier millenia
of preparation, there emerged the first human
soul, and a man breathed, and wondered, and
worshipped.

The late Sir Ernest Shackleton recorded that
in his last Antarctic expedition, when he and
two companions were making a forced march
of thirty-six hours, through the awful perils of
a frozen, unknown land, they all became sure
of the presence of a fourth traveller, moving
unseen by their side for their strength and stay
(*South*, p. 164). So in a yet fuller and more
wonderful manner, one after another the
Shepherds became aware of a being from
another sphere standing just outside their circle,
listening. Their drawing together in meditation
and song brought them all into the same conviction about him. And at last they saw above

and around them the Glory of the Lord, in the centre of which the leaping flames of their fire seemed now but sparks. Into their hearts came the tidings of great joy, the news for which they and others like-minded had been waiting so eagerly. It may be the words of the message were all within themselves, and only the thought was transmitted to crown their midnight talk and prayer. But they knew God was speaking to them.

Suddenly there was with the angel, who, it is said, *stood by them, a multitude of the heavenly host.* As at twilight in an unlighted room a flame will, in a moment, break out from a black coal-fire and illumine ceiling and walls and every furnishing, so the earth seemed suddenly inundated with light. There were heavenly beings all about the Shepherds. Up past the sheepfold, covering the fields and the hillsides, far away towards the desert and the Jordan valley, they crowded the landscape with their splendour. And they were praising God.

Just what they sang we can hardly tell. One suspects that our English versions, with their several marginal alternatives, transmit an original doubt, lying beyond both Greek and Aramaic. For the angels were singing not to men but to God. And what may be the language of worlds higher than ours, who shall say? It must transcend all earthly dialects, as truly as our English speech transcends the chatter of monkeys in a forest. But the central fact is that the Elect Shepherds did overhear for a moment the worship of sinless hosts, and that that worship interpreted itself in their minds as a garment of praise woven of two strands—the Glory of God and the Peace of Man.

So the angels sang, and then ceased, and the Shepherds heard no more. The glory contracted, narrowed into a stream of silver that passed along those hills, and faded into the light of splendid stars, and all the earth was dark and still, except for the leaping fire of the bivouac and the tinkle of a sheep-bell.

Elect Shepherds these men most evidently were, for our records tell of no one else who saw and heard what was given to them. And yet in that land men often travelled by night. Others at that very hour may have been crossing over those Bethlehem downs and been unaware of anything of unusual spiritual import. It is true that Revelation to us men is always sacramental, and some outward token may have been common to a worldly-minded Jew and to the Shepherds: but the inward experience, the miracle, was for the Shepherds alone. Mr Charles Doughty has an entry in his *Wanderings in Arabia* which illustrates the point: " The night closed in darkly over us, with thick clouds and falling weather. It lightened at once upon three sides without thunder. The nomad people said, ' It is the angels! '—their word made me muse of the nomads' vision in the field of Bethlehem."

But our New Testament yields us a better illustration. Once in the last days of the Ministry of our Lord, in a tense moment of Calvary-anticipation, He prayed, *Father, Glorify Thy Name.* And then the evangelist adds, *There came therefore a voice out of heaven, saying, I have both glorified it, and will glorify it again. The multitude therefore, that stood by, and heard it, said that it had thundered: others said, An angel hath spoken to Him.* What to some was only a peal of thunder, to others was an angel's cry, while to our Lord, and, perhaps, to His servant John, there was an articulate voice of the Father. For in God's world every man's hearing is according to his habits of listening, and only the pure in heart see God.

In vain shalt thou, or any, call
   The spirits from their golden day,
   Except, like them, thou too canst say,
My spirit is at peace with all.
They haunt the silence of the breast,
   Imaginations calm and fair,
   The memory like a cloudless air,
The conscience as a sea at rest:
But when the heart is full of din,
   And doubt beside the portal waits,
   They can but listen at the gates,
And hear the household jar within.

So had I been travelling to Bethlehem that cold night, while the Shepherds watched, should I have heard anything but some troubling of the winds, or seen anything but some play of lightning over the fields? Had I caught sight of the Shepherds presently running along the hill towards the sleeping town, might I not have said merely: What ails those men? Is it a wolf they are pursuing?

What hinders me now from being of the company of the Elect Shepherds? Nothing but this, that I do not put first the kingdom of God and His righteousness, and my own material concerns second. There are many ministering spirits awaiting that indispensable condition of the fulfilment of their ministry to me.

The Universe is no mere collection of Stars. There is no void anywhere. To think that there is nothing where we see nothing is to convict ourselves of egotism. It is a rational belief which regards the sum of visible things as possessing an invisible counterpart. The same motive which led the Great Father to create mankind, the impulse to fashion happy, living beings, must ever have been filling the heavenly places with races of intelligence and of love. An eminent biologist, the late Professor Laycock, declared as his own firm belief: " Man is at the foot of another scale of beings, the highest of which transcends man at least as far as man transcends the zoophyte."

To-day, face to face with all the ruin and sorrow which the denial of the Christian Evangel by Europeans has involved, our faith is yet more confident that the higher rule of the Universe is love—love

That moves the sun in heaven and all the stars.

To be of the order of the Elect Shepherds is to serve a better temple and to prepare better sacrifices than, until their vision, the Bethlehem herdsmen knew. It is to minister to those vast numbers of people around us who see so little and are capable of seeing so much. It is to build up for God a nobler earthly Society than the world has yet seen, while,

With Angels and Archangels, and with all the company of heaven, we laud and magnify His glorious Name; evermore praising Him, and saying, Holy, holy, holy, Lord God of Hosts, heaven and earth are full of Thy glory. Glory be to Thee, O Lord most High.

JESUS CHRIST

I

HIS BOYHOOD

THE boy Jesus tarried behind—so, with true insight the English Revised Version renders S. Luke's significant statement concerning our Lord's Passover visit with his parents to the Temple in Jerusalem; the boy, not the child, for surely when you are twelve years old you are entitled to be called either boy or girl. Jesus lived a true life as boy, youth, man. He shewed natural instincts, learning as we learn, growing as we grow, and at last being made *perfect*, that is full grown, *through suffering*.

Milton in his *Paradise Regained* (I. 201 ff.) pictures our Lord looking back upon His boyhood thus,

When I was yet a child, no childish play
To me was pleasing; all my mind was set
Serious to learn and know, and thence to do,
What might be public good.

Milton was probably thinking of his own boyhood. He was certainly wrong about the boyhood of Jesus. We have only this one authentic story concerning those early days of our Lord, but it is given for two purposes—to shew us what His boyhood was like and to point forward to His future vocation. It is a crisis-story and shews Him standing at cross roads. Its first significance is the very contradiction of Milton.

The trouble over the losing and finding of Jesus lasted three days. The first was the day after the final Passover Service. On that day, before the sun leaped from the gap between the hills, Mary, Joseph and their Son were astir and busy. With their Galilean neighbours they gathered at one of the city gates. The mules were prepared for the women. The camels knelt to be laden with the baggage. Last purchases were made of lemons, corncakes, and water in great bulging, swaying skins. Then, as the sun mounted higher, and the streets became more crowded with traders and craftsmen, the long line of pilgrims moved through the gate, setting out on their northward journey and singing as they went one of the Songs of the Ascents,

They that trust in the Lord
Are as Mount Zion, which cannot be moved, but
    abideth for ever.
As the mountains are round about Jerusalem,
So the Lord is round about His people,
From this time forth and for evermore.

So I see these devout folk leaving the narrow streets in the deep shadows and sword-thrusts of early sunlight, passing out into the blaze of the open country, the women and children first, the men a little later with the baggage and the tents.

The sun slanted to the left of the caravan and the day wore away. At evening the whole company halted on some sheltered spot. The men pitched the tents and watered the camels and mules, setting the poor beasts free for awhile to find what herbage they might. The women prepared the supper. The few children in the party gathered one by one to their mothers. But Jesus did not come to Mary. Joseph came to his wife's tent but Jesus was not with him. Joseph said he had not seen Him all day. Then with instant alarm Mary left her preparations for the night, and, with her husband, went from tent to tent, enquiring " Have ye seen the boy Jesus?" They climbed to the hill-top near by and called aloud His name. There was no answer. Night was quickly falling. The land was growing still, except for a far-off jackal's wailing and the fearful cry of a hyaena and the forlorn dropping note of the owl. " Jesus is lost," cried Mary.

The moon did not rise until somewhat late. No search therefore could be made far from the camp. And these distracted parents had no idea that Jesus was still in Jerusalem. They could only go back, step by step, enquiring in every village along the route they had followed during the day. For this purpose it was essential they should wait for light.

What a night it was! How long! What sleeplessness and distress and sobbing and praying! "Jesus is even now devoured by some wild beast," they said. Then, when at last day dawned, they set out slowly, journeying back along the familiar road, asking of every traveller and at each khan, "Have ye seen the boy Jesus of the Nazareth party?" until at length at the close of the second day once more they saw the walls of Jerusalem. With what different feelings they now looked upon them from those which stirred their words to Jesus when first they came as they shewed Him *Mount Zion on the sides of the North, the city of the Great King.*

So a second day passed, and far into the second night, wherever lights were shewn in the houses, there Joseph and Mary, worn and haggard, went asking, as they had asked before, "Have ye seen the boy Jesus from Nazareth?"

almost refusing to take No for an answer.
" Somebody must have seen him," they said.

And it came to pass, after three days, i.e. on
the third day, *they found Him in the Temple,*
in one of the Schools there, learning with other
boys, one of whom may have been a boy named
Saul, whose home was at Tarsus across the sea.
And when they found Him, Jesus was astonishing
His masters and all His class-mates by the depth
and subtlety of His answers and questions.

How had He come there? Now it would be
an unhappy mistake and a gratuitous assumption if we thought He had deliberately chosen
to leave His parents, without their permission,
that He might seek the Temple Courts. No
technically religious impulse can excuse the
breach of human obligation. But such was not
the manner of Jesus. Evidently what happened
was this: in the bustle and confusion incidental
to the departure of the many pilgrims in different caravans, proceeding to all parts of the
country, He had become separated from His
friends, and had failed to find them, search
where He might.

At the same time there is a good deal in this
statement of S. Luke—*the boy Jesus tarried behind.*
For that is what boys so commonly do, and this

without any wilful misconduct or culpable thoughtlessness. If you take a very small boy out for a walk in the country, usually, like your pet dog, he travels double the distance you do. Now he is a motor car rushing by with an alarming change of gear, or again he is a railway engine of more stately speed and sound. If he is ten or twelve years old he will be climbing trees ahead of you, and hailing you unexpectedly from the branches; or he will be far behind, lingering over some bank of earth, where he thinks he has found a little gold mine, although it is only a heap of mica-schist; or again he is digging in a pile of way-side stones for fossil ammonites. Generally speaking, when a boy is journeying with you upon a country road, his most usual habit, if he is not far ahead, is tarrying behind. And sensible parents take the risks in this and do not sharply curtail a boy's liberty of exploration.

Now boys and girls are much the same in all ages. Homer's *Iliad* has a reference to children making sand castles on the sea-shore (xv. 362 f.) just as our children do at Margate or Bournemouth to-day. Our Lord once spoke of the children of His time playing at weddings and funerals in the market-places of Galilee, and do I not remember sometimes playing at being dead (!) when I was a small boy? That Jesus tasted the joy of games and especially of open-air adventures is a most assured deduction from any true estimate of His Humanity.

Then also we may safely classify Joseph and Mary amongst the sensible parents to whom I have referred. Jesus had never been on a long journey with them before, but on many a shorter one, and, boy-like, without any disobedience, He had often tarried behind. Had it not been so, they would never have been content to go a day's journey without seeing Him, or enquiring for Him.

I am sure His boyhood was very intense. There was always something interesting happening in the country, when Mary took Him with her to visit her friends at Cana. He would cry out with joy over the lilies of the field and then check Himself in wonder and reverence. His sense of charm in the rocks and hills and long roads that led to the world's great cities, His love of talking to people, to the merchants about their camels, their bales and as to what Egypt was like and the great river there— all these boyish activities and enthusiasms and excursions Mary well understood. And on all previous occasions of their country travels He had come home safely at nightfall, sometimes hungry enough, for He had had nothing to eat all day, but He had seen so much, and, He eagerly asked, did His mother know that the rock doves were building just under the crag by the road to Capernaum? and might He go to the Sea of Galilee some day, for were there not many fishing boats there? So then all through that first day of the return to Nazareth, whenever she thought of her boy, Mary smiled to herself and guessed that He would be seated on some huge pile of baggage, talking to the herdsmen or searching for new wild flowers along the road, and so she had not been anxious at all.

Now when Mary and Joseph had to turn back to find Him it is evident they did not at once go to the Temple. The narrative implies that they went there as a last resort, scarcely hoping for success. For is it not written *And when they saw Him, they were astonished*? If Jesus had been much given to pious talk—as healthy boys never are—they would have said, " If He is anywhere in the city He will be in the Temple: He is so fond of Rabbis." But I believe that up to that time His communion with the

M 2

Father had been a still pool hidden away within granite walls of reserve, with very little over-flow into the stream-courses of ordinary conversation. So Mary and Joseph did not think of the Temple School as at all a likely place in which to find Him. I believe they went to Antonia Castle and asked in the guard-room, and to the walls of the city, and to the gates and to the markets and to the Pool of Siloam—for He would be wanting to watch the dripping trickles fall from the dark rock tunnel above, and to Bethesda—for He would wait to see the angel feet descend upon its waters, and, likely enough, then be eagerly helping some poor, diseased person into the pool. And at last in despair they said, "We can but try the Rabbis' School in the Temple," and then when they saw Him there they were astonished.

I have found this to be a crisis-story, looking both behind and before. But Joseph and Mary did not realise the prospective quality of this happening. In their astonishment they were thinking of Him in the light of the past alone. They had not dreamed that the boy Jesus would that day begin to put away boyish things and set Himself to Life's serious business. But we, knowing the things that came after, and seeing the Divine Manhood that gradually grew out of stainless, eager boyhood, can understand how, on that day, when He missed His parents amid the crush of departing caravans, and could not find them, and asked Himself where He should go and what He should do, the sense of His future calling came faintly stealing over His boyish spirit, and drew Him aside to the Temple School, with the idea of immediately beginning to prepare for His life-work, while He awaited His parents' return. And we can understand too, that this was something new in Him, something which even Mary did not at once grasp, something unlike what He had been. " How is it that ye sought me, so painfully and sorrowfully? Wist ye not that I must be in my Father's house? Did you not guess that if I missed you and could not find you I should come here?" No: *they understood not the saying which He spake unto them.* To them His answer was like that of another Jesus than the boy whose interests and tendencies had always seemed concerned with less solemn things.

Now when we are grown-up people and cast back in our minds, can we not often remember a day when there came a surge of new life into

2-2

our consciousness and we put away our tin
soldiers, or dolls, and stretched out our hand
with conscious power to an adult act? And
when also, being grown up, we begin to watch
other child-life and to chronicle its phases,
sometimes we come suddenly upon a hidden
blossom where we had never before discerned
a bud, though we had thought we knew all
the buds, and we ask ourselves, What does
this mean? What is he going to be? So was
it with Jesus on that day. He suddenly passed
out of Boyhood, and Mary and Joseph were
astonished.

Yet after all He did not so much pass out
of Boyhood as pass with His Boyhood into
Youth and Manhood. A Chinese philosopher
(Mencius) has said, " The great Man is he who
does not lose his child's heart." And I can see
that the boy temperament remained with Jesus
all His days. I think He often recalled the
beauty of the first lizard He saw, His earliest
glimpse of the sea, a sight of Hermon over-
topping all the hills. Men have emphasised the
inwardness of His teachings. I see it, but I am
impressed also with the mirroring of the objective world in His discourses. A man's metaphors
shew the habits of his eyes. And Jesus spoke as

He had looked, and loved to look upon this busy world and the teeming interests of God in Nature.

> My heart leaps up when I behold
>   A rainbow in the sky:
> So was it when my life began;
> So is it now I am a man;
> So be it when I shall grow old,
>   Or let me die!
> The child is father of the Man;
> And I could wish my days to be
> Bound each to each by natural piety.

It was not wonderful therefore, that in His public teaching Jesus should insist upon men and women needing to become boys and girls once more. He knew that a healthy child, with its games and its tarryings behind, was nearer to the right way of living than the grown man whose ambition it might be to haunt the courts of kings. He desired His hearers to be alive to the things without them, unmindful of social prestige and all the silly trouble of worldliness, caring rather for the earth and sky God had made, and, most of all, for the bringing in of His rule everywhere; that they should lose themselves to find themselves, as in a very literal way, He Himself had once lost Himself and found

Himself to the glory of God and for the service of us all.

I agree, too, with those who have seen in His teaching occasional touches of playfulness, revealing a nature which could sometimes be almost non-moral, almost secular. And personally I do not think I want, as my Leader and Ideal, One who is always sublime. I want a Christ who will walk with me and not always march. For life is not always a Mount Everest adventure. It has its long, level stretches and its seasons of commonplace. And in the Jesus, whose Boyhood so often knew the charm of wayside things, who loved to linger and see and delight in them for their own intrinsic interest, I see One whose saving grace gives me back all the lost values of our earthly life, *the hidden treasures of the sand*, as the Deuteronomic poet calls them, and I cry to Him with joy,

Jesus, divinest, when Thou most art Man.

II

HIS YOUTH

I WONDER whether there are men and women of my age who remember how in the year 1883 an enterprising firm of publishers launched Morley's Universal Library in shilling volumes of two styles: one (altogether the preferable) in plain, grey binding with paper label and the edges uncut. It was a joy on the 25th of every month to see these delightful volumes stacked in every City bookseller's shop, a joy to cut the leaves, which, like the cutting of garden-blooms, seemed to release an intenser fragrance, and it was a joy to become acquainted in these well-printed pages with some of the masterpieces of literature.

Early in the series came Goethe's *Faust* (the first part) translated by John Anster, LL.D. As I turn the leaves of my own copy, purchased at the age of 17, I see these lines underscored in pencil with evident rapture,

Yes! give me—give me back the days of Youth
Poor, yet how rich!—my glad inheritance
The inextinguishable love of Truth,
While Life's realities were all romance—

Give me, oh! give youth's passions uncon-
fined
The rush of joy that felt almost like pain,
Its hate, its love, its own tumultuous mind:—
Give me my youth again.

The underscoring shews the attestation of one
youth's experience. And it is good to be reminded, after nearly forty years, what it felt
like to be seventeen. How else shall one do
justice to the lads and lasses of that age now?
And how else shall I understand this closely
packed statement of S. Luke concerning the
youth of our Lord, *And Jesus advanced in wisdom
and stature, and in favour with God and men* (Luke
ii. 52)? Every one of those things, by which the
great German poet distinguishes youth, distin-
guished Jesus at seventeen years of age and there-
abouts—the inextinguishable love of Truth,
while Life's realities were all romance,—the
élan and spirituality that invested realities, clari-
fied by a love of Truth which nothing could
suppress: the unconfined passions which have
their deep-sunk wells in the flesh, the rush of
joy which was almost pain, hate and love (*Ye
that love the Lord, hate evil!*) and the tumultuous
mind like a highland river in spate.

He advanced in stature. It was the time when

the neighbours would say to Mary, How fast
your son is growing! She had often to weave
and make for Him new garments to replace
those outgrown. She would promise Him that
some day, when He should be as tall as Joseph,
she would make in one seamless piece a tunic
He could always wear. So He increased in
chest measurement and strength of arm. Once,
many years afterwards, in His teaching He said
playfully to the people, *Which of you by being
anxious can add one cubit unto his stature?* He was
reminiscent of the days, when it might have
been jestingly said of Him, that boyhood's
longing to be grown up was being fulfilled at
the rate of a cubit a day. In His youth He must
have been laying the foundations of future
health, because afterwards, when the full pressure of the toils of manhood was upon Him,
He bore His terrific burdens without breaking
down. His powers of endurance are often
evident to the reader of the Gospels. In His
public work He could be intensely busy, often
forfeiting His meals, and spending His nights in
prayer. The people flagged at His preaching,
and once, at least, He had to find a meal for
them in the wilderness, but there is no record
that He partook of it Himself. Physically He

must have arrested the eyes of men everywhere. The ring of health and strength was in His voice, so that the evangelists sometimes write, *Jesus cried and said.* The evil-minded shrank before Him when His anger shewed. And all these things, I say, were founded in a youth that was without weakness, slackness, vice, and that was strenuous and pure in body as in mind.

Then also, *He advanced in wisdom.* Now the Hebrew conception of Wisdom is very rich. *The Lord spake unto Moses, saying, See, I have called by name Bezalel....and I have filled him with the Spirit of God, in wisdom, and in understanding, and in knowledge, and in all manner of workmanship, to devise cunning works, to work in gold, and in silver, and in brass, and in cutting of stones for setting, and in carving of wood, to work in all manner of workmanship* (Ex. xxxi. 1). So too the wisdom of Jesus included artistic and aesthetic elements. His life was rich in seeing and in the mastery of tools. He had the Spirit of God for the creation and execution of a beautiful design.

It is certain that He read much. Unlike some of His followers, whose boast it is that the Bible is all they need, Jesus read outside the sacred Canon. For the Hebrew people did not cease to write noble books when the Old

Testament was complete. There were works which would be accounted modern in the youth of Jesus, authentic traces of which may be seen in His teaching. I mean especially *Enoch, Sirach, The Wisdom of Solomon*, and *The Testaments of the Twelve Patriarchs*. He read, for He had an open mind. But His mind's openness was not like a door that ever stands open to the street, admitting all the litter and odds and ends careless passers-by may cast away and the winds blow in. The open mind should be an active mind. And His was a mind that could sift and divide, taking in all the truths He could attest and use in the upbuilding of Himself, and casting away, like the shavings of His joinery, the mere fancies and wildnesses of the age. This is wisdom. It is the working of the Spirit of God. And it comes to him who prays.

I must pray more than I do. I am often tempted to grudge time from my books for the pursuits of prayer. But unless I pray whole-heartedly and largely my books will profit me nothing.

It was thus Jesus prepared to minister as a full man to a many-sided human life around Him; as a Master of Life caring for all things that are *true, pure, lovely, and of good report,* not as an expert whose specific knowledge is unrelated to the broad fields of human activity.

There was yet another advancement of Jesus in the days of His youth. *He advanced in favour with God and men.* Now that is a very difficult statement. I believe there is only one way in which it can be rightly read, but that when it is so read one gets therefrom a view of the beauty and unity of His youth.

The difficulty is this: is it possible for any one to advance at the same time in favour with God and men? Experience too often shews that as one grows in favour with men he grows out of favour with God. *Woe unto you, when all men shall speak well of you! for in the same manner did their fathers to the false prophets.* S. James puts the matter pithily thus, *The friendship of the world is enmity with God.* And the converse often holds good: *The Servant of the Lord is as a root out of a dry ground: he hath no form nor comeliness; and when we see him, there is no beauty that we should desire him.*

In the youth of Jesus there were many distressing social corruptions even amongst the godly. There were unjust judges, unrighteous stewards, careless and slothful porters, husbandmen who were Bolsheviks, burglars working at night, folk who promised and failed to perform.

Also we read of divorce-questions, the symptoms of ruined homes and broken vows. Nazareth, no doubt, had its full share of the world's evil ways. Can any good thing come out of it? asked an upright man who lived only four miles away. To grow in favour with the men of Nazareth and at the same time in favour with God—how should such a thing be?

There were thorny, political questions, too, in those days, movements of parties, out-breakings of revolt, and many a cruel deed done in the name of order, or in that of liberty. It was a time when so far as a youth had both stature and ability he would likely be drawn to take sides, and then, alas for piety! A side is ever a partial thing, and often an unjust thing. And young men when they take sides generally sin against Justice, even when most animated against what is unjust. One of the shrewdest of Englishmen, Francis Bacon, observed, " Young men, in the conduct and manage of actions, embrace more than they can hold, stir more than they can quiet; fly to the end without consideration of the means and degrees; pursue some few principles, which they have chanced upon, absurdly; care not (hesi-tate not) to innovate which draws unknown inconveniences, use extreme remedies at first, and that which doubleth all errors, will not acknowledge or retract them; like an unready horse, that will neither stop nor turn." (My copy of *The Essays* is also in that same excellent Universal Library to which I have referred at the outset, and I find in it that this passage also is marked with approbation though less heavily, and so I suppose one youth at least has admitted the truth of the indictment.)

In the tumultuousness of the youthful mind, in passions of hate and love how did it happen that Jesus pleased both God and men? That He kept Himself unsullied and yet winsome, His Life a thing the Holy God and the sinful world could both delight in, was surely due to the exercise of self-restraint. It was because He held back from expressing judgment, or taking sides, that His youth fascinated alike the good and the worldly. For is it not clear that youth is God's appointed season for the acquisition of such self-restraint, and is the only time, after childhood, when, in the average conditions of a sinful world, it is possible for any one to advance in favour with both God and the generality of men? In youth especially, that other word of S. James, learnt perhaps in the Nazareth home, is a timely word, *Be swift to hear, slow to speak, slow to wrath.* It is the very tumultuousness of the rapidly growing mind which disqualifies it for the expression of judgment. I may see visions without seeing men as they are. And in a week I may fortify one position after another, to abandon each for yet another more eminent. I am sure there were many things in Galilee about which Jesus in His youthful zeal felt strongly. But the consciousness of the onward sweep of His mind kept Him silent. The thought-distances He traversed day by day were too vast for the focusing of judgment, and while others were loud in protestation I think He prayed, as the Psalmists sometimes did,

> *Set a watch, O Lord, before my mouth;*
> *Keep the door of my lips.*
> *I will take heed to my ways,*
> *That I sin not with my tongue:*
> *I will keep my mouth with a bridle,*
> *While the wicked is before me.*

So He was *dumb with silence* and held His peace *even from good.* He would say, I shall see it more clearly when I am older, when the days of immaturity are past.

Thus when Manhood came there were no

excrescences of Soul to be taken over from the days of youth—no prejudices, nor habits of hasty and provoking speech, nor any ways of insolence towards those of greater experience, nor any parading of learning. And so it was that when at last He broke His long silence, the people who had known His upbringing wondered at the words of grace which proceeded out of His mouth. And they said, *Is not this Joseph's son?* They rubbed their eyes and looked at one another blankly. "*What is the wisdom,* they said, *that is given unto this man? Is not this the builder?* We have known Him all our lives. We were pleased with Him just because He was one of ourselves. We liked Him for His quiet ways."

They erred, no doubt, in the interpretation they put upon His quietness. But their amazement when He did speak in public reveals what His demeanour had ever been in the days when He had been feeling most intensely and thinking, as we say, furiously,—*swift to hear, slow to speak, slow to wrath.* And that was indeed a very wonderful mastery of youth's tumultuous mind, such a mastery as both God and men must applaud. For the motive of it was the will to be just.

The great achievement of the human mind
Is the idea of Justice. More than arts
And sciences, than faiths and rituals, this
Lifts all our Life above the life of beasts.
Chiefly by this are we a nobler kind,
The Earth's elect and separate; lost to this,
Our State is as the state of beasts indeed,
That snatch their meat, one from another's
    mouth,
And without pain another's pain behold;
Though these are guiltless, knowing not light
    or law[1].

I find few people who have shared in this achievement, because few have desired to be just despite themselves. The trouble generally goes back to the wild-oats period of life. And because in our youth we cannot hold our tongues, in our manhood we are without magnanimity. Unlike the great Master we cannot see beyond the little place in which with puny arm we fight for a party or shibboleth. We have no sight of a great Last Day. And if we do not often change our sides we often have to eat our words. But He built the finality of His word in deeps of Silence.

[1] Sir Wm. Watson's *For England*.

M   3

III

HIS ARTISAN LIFE

Is not this the tektōn? the people of Nazareth asked concerning Jesus. Now a *tektōn* was any worker in wood, horn, metal or stone. He might be a carpenter. He might be a stone-mason or a builder. The traditional saying of Jesus, *Raise the stone and there thou shalt find Me, cleave the wood and there am I,* would seem to be reminiscent of two branches of the same calling. It is significant that Joseph, who also was a *tektōn,* was connected with Bethlehem, which for many ages was identified with the stone-mason's craft.

I read the question of the neighbours of Jesus, therefore, as, *Is not this the builder?* that being the larger meaning of the word. As both carpenter and stone-mason, He would be a maker of cradles and of the burial-bier, a hewer of stone in quarries, a builder of houses. And the hard toiling at these tasks, mostly carried on in the open air, would help to crown His youth's continence with the robust muscularity of a perfectly healthy man.

What, in the light of His subsequent ministry,

may I gather as to the character of these sixteen or seventeen years when He was known either as the builder's son, or as the builder himself?

1. The first thing I see is that in the management of His workman's life He was thrifty, and this for a purpose. I believe He was well-paid, for during all that time, and much later, there were big building operations going on at the Temple in Jerusalem, and the Temple-artisans had good wages, and must have set some sort of standard for wages throughout the country. Galilee was a healthy and a prosperous province, and work was plentiful. So as the years went by Jesus was surely able to save a considerable sum of money. And that He did save is evident from the facts of His career. He was a recognised householder of Capernaum. And it is in keeping with this that in the last year of His Ministry the collectors of the Temple Tax applied to Him there for His contribution.

He established and kept that home in Capernaum not chiefly for Himself, but for His mother, and, possibly, for His sisters. He had very strong opinions about the duty of a son towards the support of his parents, and once sternly reproached the Pharisees for substituting so-called religious for filial benevolence. At

3-2

the Cross He commended His mother to the keeping of the beloved disciple, in doing which He clearly shewed that up to that time he had kept her Himself. Now, that He was able to support Mary in the Capernaum home during the years when He was no longer toiling at His craft, can only have been due to steady hard work and thrifty habits all the time when as a builder He was getting good money.

On the other hand, I believe we commonly overwork that tragic saying, *The foxes have holes, and the birds of the air have nests; but the Son of Man hath not where to lay His head.* His homelessness at the time[1] when He let fall this pathetic lament was not due to lack of means, but to the enmity of those from whom He had often to hide Himself, and who at last crucified Him. But He was not always in so miserable a plight. If, at any time, He was short of money, it would be because He was reluctant to draw upon the savings He had gathered for the upkeep of that little home by the sea, where His mother lived and often listened for His returning footsteps. Certainly it would be a mistake to think of the Twelve and their Lord as mendi-

---

[1] There can be no doubt S. Luke preserves a better context for this saying than S. Matthew.

cants. They had a common bag. They gave to the poor. We may be sure the builder amongst them would not give the least.

So His artisan life must have been a life of careful thrift, in expectation of a time when He could afford to exchange it for that of an unpaid worker of altogether a different kind. And because of this, when that time came He could honestly teach the poorer folk who gathered about Him to trust the Father. When He pointed them to the birds, *which neither sow nor reap, and have neither store chamber nor barn*, it was not, as some have foolishly thought, that He deprecated our laying by for days to come, but that if God took care of such thriftless creatures as the birds, how much more would He be likely to provide for His own children who, with all their honest toil, yet found it hard to make two ends meet. Jesus practised thrift and made a virtue from it.

2. Then I see, too, that in His builder's work He must have been faithful. The Moravian Church liturgy rightly prays, "May Thy faithfulness in Thy handicraft make us faithful in our share of labour." True, there is no Scripture that speaks of the honesty of His work. That is hardly to be looked for. The Gospels seldom

praise Him. I believe the Evangelists would
have felt it an impertinence to say, "Now Jesus
wrought honestly at His handicraft." The
apostolic emphasis upon honesty is sufficiently
indicated by the story of Ananias and Sapphira.
No one, who knew the Lord in the days of His
flesh, would ever have dreamed of enquiring
concerning the quality of the work He did in
building and in making.

It is, however, worth our while to consider
this inevitable honesty in Jesus, because it
belongs to the unity of His character.

> For His work by axe and saw
> Would be all without a flaw,
> Like His patience upon Calvary
> To magnify the Law.
>
> Very dear the Cross of shame
> Where He took the sinner's blame,
> And the tomb wherein the Saviour lay,
> Until the third day came;
> Yet He bore the self-same load,
> And He went the same high road,
> When the carpenter of Nazareth
> Made common things for God[1].

Every one's life is a unity of some sort. Our
work, be it manual or mental, reacts upon our
spiritual attitude. Nothing so soon comes back
upon the mind of a mechanic with disastrous

[1] Walter C. Smith's *Poems*.

effect as bad workmanship. A slipshod crafts-
man could never be an accurate thinker.
A tradesman who gives scanty measure is
always an unbeliever, whatever words he may
use, or misuse. And, on the other hand, Truth
comes to men through the common plain
virtues, however inarticulate the doer of them
may be in avowing faith.

I take up the teaching of Jesus and at once
I am impressed with the severity of His mind—
a mind which would be an impossibility in a
dishonest workman. What an edge there is upon
His sayings! What a fine scorn, as He describes
I fear too many of us feckless make-it-do people!
The patch on an old garment, the misuse of old
wine skins, the building of a house without
proper foundations, the lazy hopefulness concerning a half-filled lamp, the loins ungirt—all
these scorns of Jesus, and, with them, the
strenuous note that bids us brace ourselves for
work in the house after a day's hard toil in the
field, or courageously take up a cross day by
day—all these, I say, are not the thoughts of
a man who would use green timber for seasoned,
or daub with badly-tempered mortar, or be too
careless to use a plumb-line. No: just as there
is no haste in His words, no saying of His we
have to unsay for Him, so we may be sure in

those days of His artisan life there were no loose touches of the hammer and chisel as He wrought in stone or wood, no unfinished edges that might tear the user's hand. And just because He was a workman not needing to be ashamed, He was qualified to speak of the things that concern God. Through the long years of His builder's toil this maker of earthly houses learnt how to build also houses not made with hands, in that City which hath foundations whose architect and builder is God.

3. Yet He would never have built in that City had it not been for a third characteristic of His artisan life—His mind was not caged by His calling.

It is generally and rightly believed that manual labour was held in honour by the Jews of our Lord's time, yet it was also felt that for Divine learning men needed at least leisure, and it was not realised that craftsmanship might have its beneficent reactions upon the mind— a truth which, perhaps, we owe in part to modern physiology. In one of those extra-canonical books Jesus had read, I mean that by His namesake, the son of Sirach, there is a long passage repudiating the idea that workmen could ever be men of counsel or of religious instruction. Here are a few sentences:

The wisdom of the scribe cometh by opportunity
  of leisure:
And he that hath little business shall become wise.
How shall he become wise that holdeth the
  plough,
That glorieth in the shaft of the goad,
That driveth oxen, and is occupied in their
  labours,
And whose discourse is of the stock of bulls?
He will set his heart upon turning his furrows;
And his wakefulness is to give his heifers their
  fodder.
So is every *tektōn* and workmaster,
That passeth his time by night as by day.

The son of Sirach then goes on to enumerate
the lapidary, the smith and the potter as other
types of manual workers:

All these put their trust in their hands;
And each becometh wise in his own work.
Without them a city cannot be inhabited,
And men shall not sojourn nor walk up and
  down therein.
But they shall not be inquired of for public
  counsel,
And they do not understand the covenant of
  judgment;
Neither do they declare instruction and judg-
  ment;
And where parables are they shall not be found.

So little did Jesus the son of Sirach foresee
the career of Jesus the *tektōn* of Nazareth. And

what he wrote in the second century before Christ, many of our Lord's own contemporaries endorsed. *Whence hath this man these things? And what is the wisdom that is given unto this man? Is not this the tektōn?...How knoweth this man letters, having never learned?* And was there not some truth in all this? How often I find myself sadly quoting the old proverb, *Ars longa, vita brevis!* All too few are the hours for brooding or for reading.

And further, one has to add to the apparent wisdom of Sirach the admission that there is often also a bad reaction of work upon the mind. It meets us in all walks of life. The professor at the breakfast table is a person I cannot endure. Still less can I put up with the manufacturer who can only talk of "costings," or the stock-broker with his tales of "bulls" and "bears." Then,

> I want to know a butcher paints,
> A baker rhymes for his pursuit,
> Candlestick maker much acquaints
> His soul with song, or, haply mute,
> Blows out his brains upon the flute![1]

We moderns owe much to Samuel Butler for his *Erewhon* with its protest against the machines and their tyranny. Everyday the justice of that book becomes more grimly clear. For men are the victims of the works of their hands. And

[1] *Shop*, Robert Browning.

that is defeat of soul where one should be more than conqueror. Misuse! misuse! I see it every day, the misuse of God's ordinances, and the upside-downness of the world after men have taken charge of it. Handiwork and all honest toiling is an ordinance of the Spirit, for the discipline of character and for the conjoining of moral things with things of the intellect, for the procuring from the body of its quota towards personality and the fusing of flesh and spirit in the liberty of the glory of the Children of God. But how far are we from this!

All this, however, was the technique of the *tektōn* to Jesus. But beyond all the healthy reaction of His work was the superb escape of His Spirit. His mind was in no sense caged by His calling. It had a far-flung reach. He had both tactics and strategy. He could confine Himself for the time to the quest of the lost sheep of the house of Israel, while yet looking for His Gospel to be preached in all the world and to the end of Time. He lived and wrought at common tasks in an unshadowed consciousness of God; and from His tools and His designs His workshop and His quarry, there came gifts that gave ballast to the thought-ships He set sailing upon the Infinite Sea.

IV

HIS BAPTISM

D<small>R RENDEL HARRIS</small> in his *Life of F. W. Crossley* ("S. Francis of Ancoats, whom we count as real a saint as S. Francis of Assisi") relates of him the following incident:

Upon one notable occasion, when he was on the bench of magistrates (for he was now a Justice of the Peace), he was called upon to take part in the trial of a Salvation Army lassie for obstructing the public thoroughfare. (What they were really obstructing was a broad road of another character for the crowding of which they were not responsible!) When the case was called, Frank Crossley left his seat on the bench, and took his stand by the side of the Army girl in the dock.

That was a very beautiful thing to do, and in all the circumstances of the case a brave thing. But the girl was morally right, if legally wrong, and something of indignation may have upheld our S. Francis as he crossed from the bench to the dock.

When our Lord went down into the Jordan to be baptized by John, in those same waters wherein sinners of all sorts including the publicans and harlots of Israel had sought to wash away their sins, He did a similar but deeper thing. He who might have judged stood down amongst the guilty. The Baptism of John was *of repentance unto remission of sins*. And Jesus who knew no sin would have been quite rightly turned away by John, had it not been that standing there, humbly waiting His turn, He stood vicariously, as He expressed it—in order *to fulfil all righteousness*.

I cannot help asking here in parenthesis, Did not our Lord by these words open a train of thought in the Baptist's mind, whereby he was led forward into a larger view of the Christ than previously he had entertained? Every reader of the Gospels must notice how the Baptist's teaching, as it is given us in the Fourth Gospel, is more spiritual and more (in our use of the word) evangelical than his teaching as it appears in the Synoptics. One is tempted to think that the Fourth Gospel here, as perhaps elsewhere, reads back into the wonderful story of Jesus the later apostolic experience. But may not the coming of Jesus to be baptised, and His striking answer to John's remonstrance as reported in S. Matthew, have altered John's entire outlook, so that, while the Synoptic picture of John and story of his work are true enough of the beginnings of the man and his mission, the Fourth Gospel may preserve an authentic note of his developing mind under the influence of Jesus? For John was, on S. Matthew's shewing, evidently startled by the Lord's coming amongst the sinners, knowing Him to be the only one who most truly needed no repentance.

However that may have been, whether or no John began then to explore the thought of vicariousness, it was certainly as a vicarious penitent Jesus stood there. Let me see Him there aright and I shall understand that wonderful saying of another John concerning Him— *the Lamb that hath been slain from the foundation of the world*.

There are three things, says a Welsh proverb, which come unawares upon a man—sleep, old-age and sin. From its initial stage onward, sin darkens the sinner's outlook. All sin begins in little things, so that the darkening is at first but a slight contraction of our sight. The Delectable Mountains we saw as children lose just a little of their firm sky-line. In the first gathering haze moral standards begin to blurr. We are not so sure in ourselves what Right is, nor how God would have us walk. Then excuses come the more readily to open the way of the pleasures of sin. We are not insincere, only slightly depraved. And there are always plenty of people ready to welcome those who have come down in the spiritual world, in contrast to our experience in the world of affairs. So what was once an eagerness to please God is discarded now as what we are pleasantly told is but a narrow scruple. Instead of doing what we feel God would have us do, our actual rule of conduct becomes conformity to the things most other people do; and to say that a thing " is not done " is sufficient reason for our ceasing to do it. And all the time every act of obedience to these lower standards casts a shadow vaster than itself upon the heights, whereon our reverent gaze had once loved to dwell. Then as in our northern clime the days darken more quickly in December than in July, so there is an acceleration in the falling of shadows about our moral pathway. The winter is upon us before we know it, and it comes at last with a leaping down from the mountains to the foothills, and from these to the very plain.

Conversely, as a man increasingly does what is good his conception of goodness heightens and clarifies, awakening in him almost a restless desire after Holiness. We even at first, if the Light is not tempered with some useful scepticism, bemoan ourselves as unworthy. Seeing our Lord in His glorious cheerfulness and evident mastery of things, we are ready to cry out, *Depart from me, for I am a sinful man, O Lord.* God lifted up amongst the Seraphim causes me to exclaim distressfully, *Woe is me! for I am undone; because I am a man of unclean lips, and I dwell in the midst of a people of unclean lips.* In fact there is no man of any progressive moral attainment who does not often feel his unworthiness.

So the moral situation is just this, that those in most peril of sin are usually least aware of their real degradation: and the man whose life is moving out of such danger has the clearest perception of what sin is.

That is a moral situation which calls for priesthood. Priest, I know, is a word which to many of us has an evil sound. But the fact of priesthoods all through the world's history is evidence of a function to be fulfilled. Every one of us needs some person of clearer moral vision, or of attained peacefulness of vision, to convict Conscience or to quiet us *whereinsoever our heart condemn us*.

It was to be such a priest that Jesus came mingling with the sinners whom John's Baptism crudely enough attempted to save. Jesus saw the people's need as they did not see it themselves. He saw men made uneasy by John's thunderous words, penitent, in a sense, but how inadequately! He saw human souls in anguish, but more fearful of the punishments of God than filled with loathing of themselves. Many, doubtless, were like that man the late Sir Fredk. Treves told of in *The Cradle of the Deep*, who, during a strange darkness upon his island home in the Indies, fearing the end of the world had come, was seen throwing into the sea a silver article he had stolen, and then later, when the darkness had passed, seeking to recover it from the waves. John's tremendous invective and prediction of nearing judgment shook all Israel, and men repented of their sins. But how imperfectly they knew themselves! How scantily they knew God! How truly their repentances needed to be repented of! "The sinner can fast," said S. Francis of Assisi, "he can pray, weep, macerate himself, but one thing he cannot do,

he cannot be faithful to God." And Jesus, with
Whom it was natural and spontaneous to love
God, saw more clearly than S. Francis the pitiful
shabbiness of popular religion, the subterfuge
and shift, and the green-room practices of a
public mission, and how much needed to be done
before the open confession of sin could really
be an act filled to the full with righteousness.
His love of God made Him zealous for the
honour of God; and that hallowing of the
name of God, for which he taught us to pray
before we pray for anything else, demanded of
Him some priestly act of intercession, through
which these faulty human prayers might really
avail for the outpouring of the Spirit.

Then just as He reaffirmed for all men the
Law of Moses, that they should love their
neighbours as themselves, so did He ever seek
to bestow His own gracious sympathy upon
those for whom He prayed. It was for them
He had come into the world. He never told
the people in any gush of sentiment, "Men and
women I love you," but all men might see that
His life was given to them. For their sakes He
had left His tools and His not unprosperous
craftsmanship and the little home He had
builded by the sea, and was about to devote

all His time to teaching and healing the people. It was love of humankind which brought Him to do this and to devote Himself deliberately and with public solemn rite to the Service of His fellows.

So as He stood in the waters He prayed, and all the circumstances of the occasion point to such a prayer as this, "Accept my sorrow for the sins and shortcomings of these Thy children. Who can understand his errors? They know Thee not, but I have known Thee and that Thou art Holy." In that moment He was truly, as the Baptist discerned, *the Lamb of God which taketh away the sin of the World*. Nor was that the only time He bore men's sins. *The burden of our sins He Himself carried in His own body to the Cross and bore it there* (1 Ep. Peter ii. 24, Weymouth's translation). He was carrying the burden all His days, and that it was heaviest at the end was partly because He was taking up men's sins upon Him all the way He came. There was never a tragic thing done in Galilee which He saw or heard of, never a cruel or licentious word spoken in His presence, but His eyes were troubled and His ears bled. And if in the days of His youth He spoke but little, He felt the more. And everywhere and always the repentings of sinners called for the offices of a Conscience better than their own, and for a grieving over sin which alone could fulfil all righteousness.

One day, in the course of a peculiarly joyous preaching tour, S. Francis of Assisi perceived some flocks of birds and turned aside a little from the road to go to them. Unaffrighted by his approach the birds gathered to him "as if to bid him welcome." And he spoke to them of their Creator and of all God had done for them. " Then the birds began to arch their necks, to spread out their wings, to open their beaks, to look at him as if to thank him, while he went up and down in their midst stroking them with the border of his tunic, sending them away at last with his blessing" (*Life of S. Francis* by Paul Sabatier, p. 176). It is, perhaps, no more than a pretty monastic story, though related by several of the original Franciscan documents. It illustrates that extraordinary influence over birds and animals which has been given to some men, and which perhaps depends a good deal upon the innocence and purity of the heart. So of our Lord it is said that in the Wilderness-Temptation *He was with the wild beasts,* evidently unharmed, though defenceless. It was not a strange thing, therefore, that in His Baptism a bird—some wild pigeon or dove—circled about His head, flashing back from its pure wings the golden light that broke through the shade of the willows on the bank. Perhaps His hand had often fed the birds of Nazareth or Capernaum. One who could frame that exquisite thought about the sparrows —*not one of them shall fall on the ground without your Father*—must have greatly loved birds and all wild things. And it was certainly an inspired suggestion which led each of the Synoptists to put in his picture of the Baptism of Jesus this flutter of pinions, and to connect it with the bestowal of the Holy Spirit upon Him, and the Voice of the Father acknowledging Him. Doubtless the voice was in His own heart and in the heart of the Baptizer, and the Spirit of God is God in His children's thoughts and feelings and purposes. But the bird is in the scene, too, because Jesus is central to all creation, and the whole drift and beat of Life is involved in the problem of redemption. It is not sinners alone He comes to save, but their world too—to reconcile all things to God. It was indeed by strokes of spiritual genius this picture of the

Baptism was painted for us in words so few, so full. All Heaven is here, the Father and the Spirit. All Earth is here, the Son and sinful men and the dumb creatures of God that share our nests with us. And Love which takes up the load of every weary creature, and cares for us all, gathers the loose ends of our prayers and makes them into those "golden chains that bind the whole round Earth about the feet of God." So I see my Lord praying, and the bird fondly circling about Him, and the Holy Spirit making a finer gold of the sunlight upon Him, and I know that here is given as in a cameo a picture of Him whose name is *Our Redeemer from Everlasting*.

V

HIS TEMPTATION

A FEW conclusions concerning our Lord's Temptation in the Wilderness may be regarded as generally received by Christian people to-day. I set them down here under four heads and then I desire to press the fact of the Temptation upon the reader's attention by noticing its somewhat startling sequel as narrated best in S. Mark's Gospel.

(1) The narratives of the Temptation recorded in S. Matthew (iv. 1–11) and S. Luke (iv. 1–13) must be based upon an account of the experience of Jesus given by Himself.

(2) The literary form of these narratives is that of the parable, for there is no mountain in existence from which all the kingdoms of the world and the glory of them, even though we limit the world to the Empire of Rome, could be seen. And being parable we may be sure that a personal devil was as much and as little involved in it as when Jesus said to S. Peter, *Get thee behind me, Satan.* In other words, though human beings may have been actors in the

drama, there was no supernatural stage required for the acting. All that really happened,
all the conflict, lay ultimately within His own
Soul, in prolonged vigil and meditation upon
the work He had undertaken.

(3) The three reported suggestions of the
devil express one persistent solicitation, just as
later, the one motive of the Lord's evangelic
work is expressed in the three parables of
S. Luke's xvth chapter, concerning treasures
lost and found. Indeed all four Gospels contain instances of this manifolding of His teachings
in parables. He used visible things as an artist
uses colours, one central idea being expressed in
a series of pictures.

(4) This one solicitation is that Jesus should
seek the fulfilment of His vocation by directly
employing worldly power, and by appealing to
worldly instincts in man. The suggestion to
make bread out of stones comes first. It is in
form, of course, an extravaganza, and belongs
to the class of sayings in which we have the
swallowing of camels or the passing of a camel
through a needle's eye. What this daring fancy
symbolises is some brilliant dramatic activity
on the Lord's part, impressive to the multitude
and suggestive of the coming of a Golden Age,

when, as had been foreshadowed by a Jewish
writer in the second century B.C., the Messianic
kingdom should be blessed with the best fruit
and " boundless stores of wheat and wine and
oil[1]." The same conception of worldly method
appears in the second incident of the parable—
the fanatic rôle on the Temple parapet. Here
is pictured the loosening of the spirit's activity
from its sane setting in the body for proselytising
purposes, as when in our own history George
Fox walked shoeless into Lichfield denounc-
ing " Woe to the Bloody City," not knowing
why except it were to win men to follow him.
Many a Jewish leader in those far-off times, by
appeals that had no moral content but wakened
zeal for Israel's political fortunes, quickened the
steps of his fellows in quest of the Kingdom to
the fulfilment of Satan's purposes rather than
of God's. Finally the *dénouement* of the Temptation lies in the last incident of the parable—I
am sure Matthew's order of the incidents is the
true one—the frontal assault free of all disguise,
*All the kingdoms of the world and the glory of them
will I give thee, if thou wilt fall down and worship
me.* Did this mean to Jesus the employment of

[1] See *The Sibylline Oracles translated from the Greek into
English Blank Verse* by M. S. Terry (lines 885–905).

military arms? None of His disciples appears to have said to Him, Explain to us the parable, or perhaps a more definitely affirmative answer might be given to this question, but all the circumstances point in this direction and I believe this was actually the hardest thing our Lord had to face.

The Temptation thus presented to us in a three-fold parable was a real one. It concerned His great longing to set up better conditions of life, and Shakespeare's play concerning Temptation, *Measure for Measure*, reminds us,

> Most dangerous
> Is that Temptation that doth goad us on
> To sin in loving virtue.

In some management of the circumstances in which He was placed, circumstances to us now unknown—was Simon the Zealot a factor in them?—Jesus was tempted to do the thing Satan willed. And *He suffered, being tempted.* Christian people have often failed to appreciate this reality of the Temptation. But what may appear to mildly spiritual persons no very searching ordeal was, in fact, something which shook the nature of Jesus to its foundations. He triumphed, but not easily. The *point d'appui* for the Evil One lay in the masterful strength of Jesus, His fulness of natural human life—

rich in blood, iron in physique, with continuous mental surge and energy, and instinct of command. It was not a temptation which would trouble a feebly good man. Later in History the same temptation beset Mohammed, who also like Jesus stands before us as one of the Sons of Strength. And the astonishing political success which followed Mohammed's surrender to the suggestion is evidence that the Devil's offer of the Kingdoms of the World and their Glory was not an idle boast—all of which, we may believe, our Lord saw quite clearly.

Such temptation was sure to come home forcibly to one constituted as Jesus was. He had an unfaltering will. There was in Him, too, a capacity for anger. He did not need that exhortation of the Psalmists which our quietists would be the better for heeding, *Ye that love the Lord, hate evil!* " There is much truth," said Dr Forsyth, " in Keim's treatment of Christ's temperament as the choleric[1]."

How far Jesus could go in the direction in which for Him temptation lay is shewn by the narratives of the Cleansing of the Temple. That event cannot be divested of vigorous action and indignation. The overthrowing of money changers' tables and of hucksters' seats, with the

[1] *The Person and Place of Jesus Christ* (p. 7).

driving out of cattle, can only have been the work of a man in the heat of anger, whom it would have been folly for ordinary folk to resist. He stopped when He did, because His indignation had swept Him up to the very frontiers that delimit the rival kingdoms of God and the World. Before Him lay that dominion of Satan, the World of the Force-Empires, into which He was ever being urged to go. I remember that of the Wilderness-Temptation it is said, *for a season the devil left Him*. We may be sure he came back again and again. Indeed Jesus said as much as this to the Apostles, when, at the Last Supper, He so graciously declared, *Ye are they which have continued with me in my temptations*. And manifestly the Tempter was at His side on that day in the last week, when the wrath of Jesus broke upon the Temple desecrators. It is not too much to say that those ten minutes of the Cleansing of the Temple were more critical for the character and destiny of Jesus than all the forty days in the Wilderness. If Jesus, as in the story of the Fourth Gospel, reached out His hand to knot a scourge of cords, Satan reached out his to beflag the gates of Hell. But,

> 'Tis one thing to be tempted, Escalus,
> Another thing to fall.

The Cleansing of the Temple shews the direction in which for Jesus temptation lay. There is nothing in the story for His disciples to regret. Jesus did not sin. But the force of His temptation throughout those stormy years of His Ministry is suggested to us here.

On a day when the Master was at His gentlest and holiest work fell a strange sequel to the Wilderness-Temptation. He was teaching and healing crowds of poor folk, His heart filled with a great compassion. Hour after hour sped by and still the people thronged and He could not so much as eat bread. His marvellous staying power upheld Him, but disciples tired. So far as numbers went His mission was proving a great success. And the eyes of all Israel had begun to centre upon this energetic Figure. A first hint of what was to be said about Him that day came when His friends went out to lay hold on Him. They declared, *He is beside Himself*. To us that reads as a shocking statement. One has to remember, however, that in Syria mental derangement has often been regarded as a sign of inspiration[1]. The Spirit of

[1] Cf. Hosea ix. 7: also Curtiss' *Primitive Semitic Religion Today*, pp. 150/1, and *The Expository Times*, xiii, 151.

the Lord was credited sometimes with strange actions. When Elijah mysteriously disappeared, the young prophets of Jericho conceived that that Spirit might have taken him up and cast him upon some mountain, or into some valley (2 Kings ii. 16). Not unkind criticism but superstitious anxiety animated the friends of Jesus.

Worse, however, was to follow. There arrived a deputation of scribes from the Temple in Jerusalem. These were men utterly unlike the simple folk whom Jesus had around Him. They were dialectical, clever men and, coming from the headquarters of the Faith, they were greeted with deference by all. Then, to the horror of His disciples, these official persons accused Jesus of having done the very thing which, as a matter of fact, He had been tempted to do. They said He had made a compact with the Evil One.

The accusation jarred tremendously. That Jesus felt and saw a startling connection between the Wilderness-Temptation and this scribal verdict about Him is clear from His words, *No one can enter into the house of the strong man, and spoil his goods, except he first bind the strong man.* As He spoke there rushed back upon Jesus the hour of that earlier battle. Had He made a compact with Satan? It was the thing which, in effect,

He had been tempted to do—not indeed, at first, nakedly, yet subtly and essentially. But these men lied. He had thrust the Tempter back. He had bound the strong man.

He was terribly moved. Should not I feel moved, if I had come faintly, though victoriously, through a most searching temptation in the recesses of my own soul, and then found myself accused of having done the very thing which, not without effort, I had rejected as a thing undivine, nay, finally diabolic? It was as though those ferret-eyed scribes had been actual witnesses of conflicts which Jesus had never dreamed any earthly being could know about. They travestied the course of His thoughts and rankly falsified the issue. But how terrible it was that they should have peered into that dark hour of His soul at all! So even in its English dress S. Mark's record of his reply reads like the story of a palpitation. There is in it a reasoning, and a certain progress of thought and feeling. His first words, *How can Satan cast out Satan?* cogent as they are, do not touch the matter to the quick as His last words do. The sentences seem to distil slowly from the alembic of a high but startled mood. Drop by drop they fall, and the last is the pure spirit of judgment. *Verily I say unto you, All their sins shall be forgiven unto the sons of men, and their blasphemies wherewith soever they shall blaspheme: but whosoever shall blaspheme against the Holy Spirit hath never forgiveness, but is guilty of an eternal sin.*

When He had finished all His teaching that day, and there gathered to Him the Twelve Apostles deeply indignant over the accusation of the Scribes, Jesus told them what the facts behind the scenes at the beginning of His Ministry really had been, told them the parable of the Wilderness-conflict very much as it lies before us to-day.

The Sequel to the Temptation raises an important question. Was it accident only that Jesus was accused of this traffic with Satan, a mere wild word almost thoughtlessly hurled at Him by men too bitter to think? Or was there some real significance in the charge?

Now from time to time God sends into the world certain commanding persons. We acknowledge in them a magnetic power, an indefinable distinction. For tens of thousands of people the late Lord Kitchener, more especially perhaps in his earlier days, possessed that quality—a quality of lonely greatness, of reserve, of authority. As is usual in such cases there are the detractors, those for whom there is only "the Kitchener legend," but Sir George Arthur's biography of the man makes his essential greatness clear to the dullest. Mr Rudyard Kipling in his poem, *Kitchener's School*, has told us how to an Oriental Mohammedan it seemed that Kitchener was mad, and this just because of his magnanimity in serving those he conquered. He was beside himself. Again and again in his career a mystery of greatness, the greatness that belongs more to instinct than to education, gathered about the man. Hence the verdict of the Eastern.

Take another type. There have been men in the Christian Church in whom the prophetic talent has been developed very remarkably by prolonged communion with God. As the years pass there shines from them a quality of goodness which inspires us with awe. When they speak, their unfolding mind is lit with the sheen of God. They seem not of this world. One who heard the late Dr Alexander McLaren in his old age address a big meeting in Edinburgh said that, as he spoke and men listened, they looked, and "it was like seeing a spirit[1]."

[1] *Dr McLaren of Manchester*, p. 189.

Such as these suggest to us somewhat the aspect of Jesus in His Galilean ministry. He was a Presence not to be put by. Men looked and looked again. His passing down the streets of Capernaum lit them with "the light that never was on sea or land." And as sicknesses melted away before Him, and words mighty, new, piercing, fell from His lips, the spell of another world was laid upon human judgment. What was it—this distinction? *What manner of man is this?* was often asked.

The verdict of the Scribes was the answer of men who almost instinctively recoiled from His teaching, as from something that was subversive of their whole manner of life, but it was not a common answer. It was in line with the verdict of His friends. Terrible as the scribal charge was it recognised the fact that here was more than a common personality. Here was something awful, transcendent, cosmic. We have to remember that in those days people did not joke about Satan. They felt and dreaded the unseen Evil Power as something gigantic, able to cast shadows over human life deep as the mountains are high. So it was not a scornful or derisive thing the Scribes said, but a thing uttered with some feeling of the reality of a world of spirit. And it did testify to this, that in Jesus was a spirit non-earthly and awful in the range of its power. As they said it, the Scribes shrank back from Him. We read He had to call them unto Him (S. Mark iii. 23) as one calls sullen and frightened children.

The Christian Church has busied itself with many Christologies, and we can learn from them all. But still the Figure of Jesus towers above us unmeasured, immeasurable. This, indeed, would seem to be the judgment of many of our best minds. On the closing pages of his book, *What is the truth about Jesus Christ?* Professor Loofs declares, "It would be attempting impossible things if we tried to understand the historical person of Christ" (p. 240). I remember, too, that He Himself said, *No one knoweth the Son save the Father.*

One thing, however, qualifies our nescience. His friends, as they approached Him a second time on that day of high momentous feeling, furnished the occasion for the one saying of His which takes the light of the mystery and brings it a little nearer to our eyes. His answer to their message was to look round about Him upon His disciples and to say, *Behold, My mother and My brethren! For whosoever shall do the will of God, the same is My brother, and sister, and mother.* Now, if it is possible by doing the will of God to become a brother of Jesus, then whatever mystery of greatness invests Him begins to invest us also. And does not that conclusion enable us to understand all we need to know about the mode of the Divine in Him?

One of the better thoughts of our modern theology is that of a progressive Incarnation. There must be degrees in any human possession of the Divine. "It should be remembered," says Dr Forsyth, "that human personality is not a ready-made thing, but it has to grow by moral exercise, and chiefly in the Kingdom of God, by prayer. The living soul has to grow into moral personality. And this should not be ignored in connection with the moral psychology of Christ. He no more than we came into the world with a completed personality—which would be not so much a miracle but a magic and a prodigy" (*op. cit.* p. 340). Step by step, as He did the will of God, the Divine was realised in Him. And it is His own word that tells us, we too, by this same practice of that will, become partakers of *the mystery of godliness.* The light of far-off worlds, the glory and spaciousness of the unnumbered ages gather about even plain men and women who walk as Jesus walked. Why need we strain our minds by vain endeavours to find a credal measure for Jesus, or trouble to fashion bonds of Church-Reunion out of fourth-century terminologies? Is it not enough that for all who do the will of God, as Jesus revealed it, the same cosmic glory, the life which is more than words can express, makes them as their Lord, according to the word of His servant John, *As He is even so are we in this world*?

VI

HIS TRANSFIGURATION

THE xvth and xvith chapters of S. Matthew, the viith and viiith of S. Mark, the ixth of S. Luke contain stories of a climax in our Lord's Galilean ministry. They shew a growth of hostility amongst the ruling classes, and signs of defection amongst the common people, and Jesus and the Twelve disposed to wander about the country with no fixed plan. Once we find our Lord as far north as the borders of Tyre and Sidon. Now I believe He went there under an impulse charged heavily with temptation. He had seen the storm clouds massing in the south. He had seen many of His disciples going back and walking no more with Him. Israel, it seemed, would have none of Him. And then the very splendour of His wider sympathies began to lure Him from the path of national service, which was to prove, in the end, His unevadable path of duty. From the first the eye of Jesus had swept beyond the frontiers of the historic home of Revelation, and had He followed His broadest thoughts He would have anticipated S. Paul's decision when he said to the Jews, *Seeing ye judge yourselves unworthy of Eternal Life, lo we turn to the Gentiles*. As the Master thus journeyed a few miles into a foreign country with the sense of exile upon Him, the very glory of that human Spirit which seems to us better than patriotism, and which has lifted Jesus above all nationalist categories, claimed Him for Mankind rather than for Israel, and appeared to make it doubtful whether His duty did not lie in the immediate service of the World rather than in continuing an unwelcome ministration to His own people. It is not always true however that our widest visions and our broadest sympathies are the allurements of the Holy Ghost. For Jesus, at this time, they were a recrudescence under a more spiritual form of the Wilderness-Temptation.

This it was, I believe, which led Him to speak so strangely to the Syro-Phoenician woman. He was seeking to bury Himself in silence, until He could fight His battle out, and settle one way or the other whether to turn to the Gentiles or to go back to His native land and resume His relinquished task. The woman who discovered His identity and sought His aid said of her daughter that she was afflicted with a devil. And well she may have been, for this appeal on her behalf was a grappling of the soul of our Master to Satan himself. Through her distressing story there was represented to Jesus the multitudinous need of the heathen world crying out for His aid. To respond to this first appeal might speedily bring upon Him others, and He be drawn finally away from Israel to serve a less violent and stubborn race. It was the realisation of this in the consciousness of Jesus which to a large extent caused that tone of roughness in his reply to the woman. He was battling with Himself when He held her off with the words, *I was not sent but unto the lost sheep of the house of Israel*, and, again, *It is not meet to take the children's bread and cast it to the dogs*.

But once more He triumphed over Temptation. He healed this one sufferer and then turned His back resolutely upon the Gentile world saying in His prayer, it may be, as once afterwards He said, *I pray not for the world, but for those whom Thou hast given me*.

It was a little later, after renewed ministry in Galilee, wherein His experience was again chequered with success and hostility, that He came to Caesarea Philippi, or Paneas as it was otherwise called. The two names of this place, the Roman and the Greek, symbolised the two dominant influences of that great heathen world by which Israel was beset.

It was originally called Paneas, because here was one of the shrines of the Greek Nature-deity, Pan. There was no more beautiful spot in that land. The town itself stood 1150 feet above sea-level. On the north-east there rose the white-capped summit of Hermon, 8000 feet higher still. Outside the town a stream 30 feet broad leaped from a dark cavern in the limestone cliff, thence rushing to join other streams in the making of Jordan. Here, amid poplar groves and clumps of oleander and occasional oak, against a background of red-brown rock, the heathen people came to worship. The grey smoke of incense and the dancing of garlanded girls to music on reed-pipes celebrated the glory of Pan, and reminded the traveller of that vast and multi-coloured mythology of Greece, which could fascinate alike the untaught peasant and the citizen of "happy glittering Athens."

But here, also, Philip the tetrarch had built a temple of white marble in honour of Augustus

Caesar, in which divine honours were paid to the greatest of the Emperors of Rome, the tetrarch renaming the town in honour alike of his master and of himself. And certainly all that Rome stood for in the ancient world was represented most worthily in Augustus, the nephew and avenger of Julius. Indomitable strength, patience, foresight, justice, liberality, and the ambition to build up the State—these were the qualities that under that noble ruler employed Roman arms in the bloody deeds of war. It was not altogether a base, if an idolatrous motive, which fashioned at the northern gateway of the land of Israel a memorial of Roman power, over against those altars that symbolised the more subtle strength of Greece.

Hither then came Jesus and the Twelve, and here, face to face with the Greek and the Roman worlds, the Lord put His challenging question, *Who say ye that I am?* evoking the enthusiastic response, *Thou art the Christ, the Son of the living God*.

Then, *from that time began Jesus to shew unto His disciples, how that He must suffer many things ... and be killed, and the third day be raised up ....* Evidently what He said created a dismay that was increased when He went on to foreshadow the Cross as awaiting all His followers. The Cross meant such a death to them as a hangman's rope means to us. Crosses enough they had seen already on many a Galilean hillock after the disastrous insurrection of Judas.

There followed a week of comparative silence. Was there some aloofness in the attitude of the Twelve to their Lord? It would not be unnatural, for all their golden hopes were smitten. At length, one evening, Jesus called to Him Peter, James, and John and asked them to go with Him to the mountain for prayer. Amid the lengthening shadows the little party set out, traversing open glades wet with dew, and entering after a time woods of pine, dry-pathed with the myriad dust of ages. Probably there was a moon and a clear sky or the climbing path would have been too dark for safety. Presently the trees became scantier and the moonlight fuller, and the travellers reached a rocky platform high up on the mountain's side. Above them they caught a glimpse of the snow-helmet of Hermon, cold beneath the sky, while the ceaseless trumpets of many waters descending from the heights proclaimed the majesty of God. The lights in distant Caesarea were dropping out. In the near south gleamed the wide waters of Merom broken at one end into reedy marsh. Farther south, hidden by the hills, lay Capernaum by the Lake, where Mary dwelt in the little stone house Jesus had built for her with His own hands and at His own expense. And, again, farther still in the dark night, He could picture Nazareth lying, His boyhood's home, a place of dreams, of endless romance, and of memories exquisitely tender.

It was now the hour of sleep, and no unusual thing for the Lord and His apostles to take their rest upon the ground in the open air. But He had come to pray, if, by the Father's loving kindness, He might confirm His own trembling purpose of suffering, and lift the incubus of disappointment from the hearts of His friends. So He knelt and for awhile the three disciples knelt with Him, until weary and heavy with sleep they wrapped their outer cloaks about them and lay down in sweet forgetfulness. Hour after hour, while they slept, and while the moon moved across the sky, while stars rose and other stars set, and the night air froze the evening dew, Jesus was wrapped in silent prayer. For such long continued devotion I fear I have little ability. We Westerns seldom have, but the Eastern Saint, even to-day, does sometimes achieve the night-long vigil. And our Lord often opened the gates of the secret garden, and passed along its paths deeper and farther than any of us ever travel. While we seldom get much beyond the entrance, He knew all its alleys and fair-bordered walks.

It is not difficult to agree with Ruskin's reading of this occasion, when he speaks of Jesus as having gone to Hermon to offer His first recorded prayer about death. Although the subject of His thoughts is not expressly declared to us, the whole narrative implies the truth of this interpretation. He had made His first clear announcement of His approaching passion and it had provoked the greatest alarm amongst His followers. In the mystic experience of the night Moses and Elijah spoke of *His decease which He was about to accomplish at Jerusalem.* And on the next day, coming down from the mountain, He enjoined the three, who had shared His vision, to speak of it to no man *save when the Son of Man should have risen again from the dead.*

So on Hermon He sought to prepare for Calvary and to carry His chief disciples with Him in this preparation. Doubtless He came to ask for strength, but, I think yet more He

came not seeking a gift so much as bringing
one. And as He gave Himself fully and utterly
to do the will of the Father, the Divine joy of
giving filled Him. He left behind the lower
stretches of the Garden and passed along its
uplands, where the paths die into the timeless
amplitudes of the spirit, and a man may have
perfect commingling with Heaven, and join
those just men who already have been made
perfect.

Is it wonderful that the exaltation of Jesus
in His praying should have magnetised into
visibility that higher hidden world which is
always over us and around, or that the love of
Jesus for the three apostles, love which is ever
an interpenetration of soul with soul, should
have broken their sleep with shafts of that
glory and voices of that speech, which in Himself were an infinite and a flawless thing? No
names were spoken; no one said to the apostles,
This is Elijah, this Moses; but intuitions leaped
into the minds of all three, that the greatest of
the law-givers and the greatest of the prophets
were with them then. Sleep was utterly gone;
their bloods flowed in racing tumults as they
looked upon the illumined Face of Jesus. The
mists that had crept up the hillsides from thick

woods of pine and cedar became luminous with a kindred beauty, as when in the old Hebrew story the Glory of God rested upon the tabernacle in the Wilderness. And in each man's inmost soul came a conviction as with a voice that pealed from God, *This is My Son, My Chosen: hear ye Him.*

Day was lighting a beacon fire upon the mountain top as the three with their Lord descended through the woods. The shadows vanished. The hill on which Caesarea was built stood up from the plain. In the marble halls of Philip's Temple an altar fire burnt leapingly to the Majesty of Rome. From that broad place of waters before the red cliff came the smoke of incense to the god Pan. But a power mightier than Rome and cleaner than Greece had been revealed in a human form. And for all time this had been made clear that the divinest thing in the World is not power to compel the reluctant obedience of men, nor even skill to weave the gossamer beauty of mythology out of our human instinct for the supernatural, but faithfulness to truth, love of love, obedience to the things of the spirit, blending in a devotion which can make of Life itself one supreme offering.

The whole story shews me the high ideal of

prayer. *As He was praying, the fashion of His countenance was altered, and His raiment became white and dazzling.* The transfiguration of a man's life comes through prayer. The more he practices it the more do faults fade out of him and graces quicken in him. His whole nature is renewed by prayer. And the inward process gradually explicates through sense, as with Edryn, who

>Slowly drew himself
Bright from his old dark life,

and whose very face with change of heart was changed.

But it is not in one fervent outcrying of soul we alter so manifestly for the better. It is in a habit of prayer we are transfigured. And this again does not necessarily mean much kneeling or an intense straining after reality. I have many duties and a busy life. I have to think hard all through the day of things to be done and to do them. But I can find some few moments every morning in which to seek my Father's Face; and again,

>Who goes to bed and doth not pray
Maketh two nights of every day.

More important than keeping the times of prayer is it to know what to say to Him. Now prayer is more than petition. The prayer which most transfigures is like our Lord's praying at Hermon, a prayer which effaces self and asks simply to be allowed to serve the Kingdom. It is not so much when we ask that God should give to us as when we ask that we might be allowed to give to Him, that beauty of Holiness outbreaks in us.

I come back, however, from these somewhat too subjective considerations to see in the story of our Lord's experience at Hermon the Divine seal resting upon His Self-sacrifice. The faith and insight that led Him to wrench Himself away from the borders of Tyre with all their vistas of a vaster world than Judaism, and which beckoned Him back to His Mission as the Redeemer of Israel, were confirmed in Him by that night of prayer. And whether I am ennobled by any sacrifice I can make or not, the thing for me to remember is my particular place of duty in the Service of God, Who knows infinitely better than I the interrelations of individual services in the great sum of earthly affairs. *Lord, what wilt Thou have me to do? Thy will be done in Earth as it is in Heaven.*

M

6

VII

HIS APOLOGIA

STEPHEN LANGTON, Archbishop of Canter-
bury, who died in the year 1228, and Robert
Stephens, a famous sixteenth-century scholar,
between them supplied us with the present
system of chapter and verse division in our
Bibles. I am much obliged to them both. Such
a system is a great convenience. Yet the price
we have paid for it, especially in the matter of
chapters, which was Langton's work, has been
heavy. For often Langton's insight was defec-
tive, and, since most Christians still blindly
follow his leading, the mess in the ditch has
been and is considerable.

I do not know any place in the Bible where
the Archbishop more strangely failed than in
the separating of the xvth chapter of S. Luke
from the xivth. The last sentence in chapter xiv
is our Saviour's word, *He that hath ears to hear,
let him hear*. The first sentence of chapter xv is,
*Now all the publicans and sinners were drawing near
unto Him for to hear Him*. The assonance of these
sentences should have revealed the continuity

of the Gospel story, and thereby would have been exhibited to us once again that genius of the third Gospel, which claims us all as sons of Adam, the Son of God.

The situation begins at verse 25 of the xivth chapter: *Now there went with Him great multitudes: and He turned, and said unto them, If any man cometh unto Me, and hateth not his own father, and mother, and wife, and children, and brethren, and sisters, yea, and his own life also, he cannot be My disciple. Whosoever doth not bear his own cross, and come after Me, cannot be My disciple.* There follow parables about counting the cost, concluding with this word, *So therefore whosoever he be of you that renounceth not all that he hath, he cannot be My disciple.* And then, to emphasise all this comes a plangent and terrible word about salt, calling for reality in all our professed sacrifices. And then, finally, in a take-it-or-leave-it tone, this austere man adds, *He that hath ears to hear, let him hear.*

A worldly person might say, "Who will wish to hear more of this sort of thing? Language like this is the way to drive people from Religion. The right aim of the teacher is attained when he gives men something like a modern Pleasant Sunday Afternoon." And look at the crowd about the Master. It is breaking up. Some of the better dressed have turned their backs and are going off to dine. But who are these edging their way into the Teacher's immediate presence? That woman does not need to be described. That man has the word " profiteer " written all over him. Yonder, in threadbare clothes, is the son of a rabbi, who has come down in the world through fast living. These, the social outcasts of Jewry, have yet ears to hear and are drawing near to hear Jesus. These are the folk who are attracted by this call for renunciation and for sacrifices that have the bitterness of salt in them. Truly our good Archbishop, by the disjection of this Scripture, lost for himself and for multitudes one of the most marvellous revelations of human nature in all the New Testament. There is a buried nobility in the basest. Speak but the word! the Evangel shall awaken Life in the lost, the hero in the slave.

I remember that exquisite story Dr John Brown tells in his *Horae Subsecivae* of Mary Duff, a poor much-sinned-against and much-sinning girl, to whom Hugh Miller, in his journalist days at Edinburgh, gave half-a-crown, seeing her bitter need, as she lay dying in her wretched garret, and who, after he had gone, rose from her bed and went through the sleet and darkness of a wintry night, to pay a last debt at her neighbour's shop, and then staggered back home to die untended and alone.

Literature has not a few such records as that and I am confident the archives of Heaven have more. But we too little reckon upon the persistence of goodness in those we say have gone to the bad.

Such were those who were actually attracted to Jesus by His most salting words about sacrifice. And He saw and rejoiced. He stood with outstretching hands to welcome them. It was the hour for dining. Philip, it may be, was unpacking the day's basket of provisions for the apostolic company. "Make the circle wider," said Jesus, "and bid our friends sit down." And they came in shyly, these down-at-heel people. And the Pharisees and the Scribes as they left whispered together, and one jerked his thumb over his shoulder, saying, *This fellow receiveth sinners and eateth with them!* But Jesus called after them, and, before they could get away from Him, in the fewest words He had drawn two pictures from life which spoke of the finding of the lost, and then, having compelled their attention, He told more at length an inimitable story on the same theme, which all the world knows as the parable of the prodigal son.

Now these three parables are the Apologia of Jesus, His defence of Himself against the suggestive sneer of His enemies concerning His attitude to wrong-doers. Like the three parables of the Wilderness-Temptation, they all have the same theme. They affirm the fitness and naturalness of His gracious bearing towards those who have gone astray and are conscious of their misery and sin. And in each parable the central figure represents Jesus Himself. The shepherd who owns the lost sheep, the woman who loses the coin, the father whose son goes to the far country—alike stand for Jesus. And in the rejoicing of which each parable speaks, the shepherd with his friends, the woman with her neighbours, the father with his household, you have the very thing set forth which Jesus was at that time doing, when He welcomed to His open-air picnic the publicans and sinners His words had found. In effect our Lord replies to the sneer of the Pharisees, "You criticise Me for rejoicing over these. Yes, I am rejoicing and My friends the angels rejoice with Me. But it is a human and beautiful thing so to rejoice, for they are Mine. And when a shepherd finds his lost sheep, when a woman finds her lost coin, when a father finds his lost son, does not the owner in each case rejoice with his friends, saying, Rejoice with me, or, It was meet to make merry and be glad? So it is natural for Me to welcome and to feast with these men and women who manifestly are responding to My call for disciples."

Now this Apologia of Jesus involves a very tremendous assertion—nothing less than His sovereignty over all flesh. Such sovereignty is indeed explicitly claimed by Him in the Fourth Gospel. But that Gospel only puts explicitly what is so charmingly assumed as a matter of course in the Synoptists, and especially in S. Luke.

Some of the medieval people had a way of speaking of our Lord which has fallen very much out of fashion now. Thus in *The Imitation of Christ*, the voice of our Lord often employs the language of a Father. S. Julian of Norwich ascribes Motherhood to Him—" Jesus Christ, That doeth good against evil, is our Very Mother: Our Father willeth, our Mother worketh, our good Lord the Holy Ghost confirmeth." And Tennyson in the *Idylls of the King* more than once introduces this parental relationship of Christ—"Our fair Father Christ."

There are inconveniences in such modes of thought but they harmonise with the New Testament view of Him. The Epistle to the Hebrews puts in His mouth the words of Isaiah, *Behold, I and the children which God hath given Me.* And then the writer goes on to say, *Since then the children are sharers in flesh and blood, He also Himself in like manner partook of the same.* That means, if it mean anything at all, they were His children before the Incarnation. He did not partake of flesh and blood in order to become human. Because He was already human—the parent of all Humanity—He partook of flesh and blood.

Here, I know, I encounter all the perplexity of the doctrines of pre-existence, and to enter upon these would take me along certain tangential lines of thought which necessarily reach very far. I come back to the simple and intelligible idea of the Parenthood of our Lord towards us all. And in doing so let me remember that Eastern ideas of parenthood emphasised authority rather than our twentieth-century idea of companionship. It was as having rights in every soul that Jesus claimed to handle men and women. That appears very clearly in the tender story of Simon the Pharisee and the woman who was a sinner. Jesus conceded that Simon was a better person than she. His sins might be symbolised as a debt of 50 pence—many of the Pharisees did in fact lead blameless lives—hers were ten times as great. But here is the striking point—both were sinners *against Jesus*. They were debtors: *He* was the Creditor. And He had forgiven both. And one loved Him little, the other much. So the parable in its application to Simon and the woman implied, as though it were a thing understood, that our Lord stood to mankind as the Eternal God, saying, Behold, all souls are Mine.

But Parenthood is not merely the symbol of authority; most clearly it means also love, which is the final idea of God. The sovereignty of Christ is the sovereignty of Love. And Love at its deepest, like Life at its swiftest, is an act of self-impartation. Indeed Life and Love at last are one. All is effluent; only the stops and self-clutchings are sin. Michelet in his *Historical View of the French Revolution*, commenting upon the divine honours paid to Louis XIV, finely remarks, "He took adoration at its word, and believed himself a God. But he comprehended nothing in that word God. To be a God is to live for all." It was thus our Lord lived—for all. Because the gross sinner was so welcomed, the upright had a lavish guarantee of acceptance. Because the publican was loved, the Pharisee in his integrity might have known the Lord loved him too. If in the parable the Father kissed his broken and ragged boy— kissed him much, says the Greek—the tenderest word of all was spoken to the boy whose life had been without stain, *Child, thou art ever with me, and all that is mine is thine.* Jesus lived for all. Even His occasional anger was a wrestling of love, never hatred. *He looked round about on them with anger, being grieved at the hardening of their hearts.*

So whoso can love most lives most, grows most into God. And just so far as we become Divine, do we acquire Divine functions. It is this which explains an utterance of the Risen Christ to which Protestants seldom do justice: *Whose soever sins ye forgive, they are forgiven unto them; whose soever sins ye retain, they are retained.* It was as men and women—for probably women were of the assembled company—who had just received an effluence from Jesus, the Lord of Love, and who were being reconstituted by Him, that they were able to forgive sins or to retain them. The authority is not sacerdotal, nor of a caste, but ethical and springs from the redeemed soul's oneness with its Redeemer. Love has entered in and made both one. And when the believer speaks, Jesus speaks. And when Jesus speaks, God speaks. *He that receiveth you receiveth Me, and he that receiveth Me receiveth Him that sent me.*

So also the *raison d'être* of authority in the commanded soul is just that persistence of goodness in us all, which our narrative reveals as a quickening of the publicans and sinners towards Jesus. It was because, though obscured by sin, there was an inherent and unalienated nobility in the basest of them—something of Jesus in them—that He had a place by right in their hearts, and they were moved to yield Him allegiance. "We are all in Him enclosed," says S. Julian of Norwich, "in us is His homeliest home, and His endless dwelling."

He has rights therefore also in me. He has Himself in me. For not only has He loved me, but through centuries of human existence by a myriad activities and institutions of Christian men He has foreshaped my life before ever consciousness awoke in me. How can I, in honour, be other than His? How can I do less than arise and come to *my Father?*

VIII

HIS MIND

I DO not propose in this section to attempt any summary or detailed description of our Lord's teaching, which would be beyond my scope and also, in view of the many text-books upon the subject, unnecessary. Rather, what I have in view is the characteristic working of His mind, what I suppose people mean to-day when they use that curious word "mentality." This, indeed, may seem a sufficiently ambitious enterprise, but what I shall set down will be what I feel God has shewn me, and I entertain no illusions as to my limited ability to receive the fulness of His word.

The Fourth Gospel, in one of its exquisite colour-touches which, as a mirror of water reflecting the expanse of Heaven, suggest to us the things of the Spirit, relates that our Lord's coat was *without seam woven from the top throughout.* That it should have been so fashioned was surely appropriate. For He who wore that seamless robe was at unity with Himself, mind and soul according well. His outward activities were the expression of an undivided mind, while His whole wonderful manhood unfolded a flawless revelation of the Eternal God.

In any study of the mind of Jesus the first thing which impresses us is, I suppose, the Inwardness of His teaching. The eye of Jesus traced moral conduct to its springs, and judged of men, not so much from what they appeared to be, as in what they truly were. *He needed not that anyone should bear witness concerning man; for He Himself knew what was in man.*

It is a commonplace that Jesus re-interpreted the Hebrew Law in terms of thought and feeling. In the Sermon on the Mount He spoke the last word upon sins of violence and of faithlessness, by shewing them as states of heart. Further, what Jesus saw to be true of men's sins He also perceived in relation to their virtues. It was from the heart, He affirmed, they were to forgive their enemies. In the heart they might offer to God real sacrifices. *Give for alms those things which are within; and behold, all things are clean unto you.*

These are practical judgments of so obvious a character that perhaps the ethic presented in them hides from us the habit of mind which is also involved. But the same mode of perception appears in more simply intellectual workings. I take as an illustration of this the parable of the good Samaritan. The remarkable thing here is that whereas our Lord's questioner had asked, *Who is my neighbour?* the answer given is through the counter-question, Whom can you be neighbour to? *Which of these three proved neighbour unto him that fell among the robbers?* The truth Jesus saw was that neighbourhood is not a physical thing, but a thing of affections, disposition, spirit. Popular speech accounts men neighbours who are outwardly proximate. Jesus said, He is my neighbour who compassionates my need. In the conventional sense and for the time being, priest and Levite and Samaritan were all alike neighbours to the wounded man, in that they all came where he was. In the view of Jesus one only proved neighbour to him, the one who helped him. He alone in deeds of pity came in spirit alongside the sufferer, so that the thoughts of the two men, the helper and the helped, blended in the closest of all proximities, love from the heart. M. Maeterlinck, who so often draws upon underlying truths of the Gospel, has well said, " To love one's neighbour in the immovable depths means to love in others that which is eternal; for one's neighbour in the truest sense of the term is that which approaches the nearest to God."

In this connection it is said of Jesus Himself, *When He saw the multitudes, He was moved with compassion for them, because they were distressed and scattered, as sheep not having a shepherd.* He saw the multitudes scattered. That does not mean He noticed that the crowds were breaking up, as a congregation of people at a service breaks up when the service is over. It means that in every assembly of persons together, where others saw a closely packed crowd, Jesus saw the same persons standing widely apart. He looked through the outward to the inward life, and, looking thus, He saw the crowds that thronged Him were scattered persons, having no bond in conscience or in hope. It is only in the affinities of the soul man comes near to man. So to be near a man in any real sense something more than physical situation is required. Here lies the justification of that inward interpretation of the Law to which I have already referred.

But what was the reason for this estimating of men by a principle of inwardness, how came He to set so much store upon what we call the heart of a man? Was it not that the inward was greater than the outward, that while the body and spirit were alike God's work, spirit was more truly representative of Him and therefore had the more abiding value? So in the parable of the Lost Son, Jesus uses the significant phrase, *When he came to himself*, or, as Wyclif rendered it, *And he turned again into himself*. The words imply something like the idea of Matthew Arnold's poem, *The Buried Life*:

Fate, which foresaw
How frivolous a baby man would be—
By what distractions he would be possessed,
How he would pour himself in every strife,
And well-nigh change his own identity—
That it might keep from his capricious play
His genuine self, and force him to obey
Even in his own despite his being's law,
Bade through the deep recesses of our breast
The unregarded river of our life
Pursue with indiscernible flow its way;
And that we should not see
The buried stream, and seem to be
Eddying at large in blind uncertainty,
Though driving on with it eternally.

The Buried Life is our more real life and is in even the Lost Son. It is this which, at last being evoked, secures his restoration. He comes to himself, that is he begins to reflect and to desire better things. The self to which he comes is more than an instinct of bodily preservation. He does better than come to his senses. For it is not only hunger he feels. He speaks of sin, and unworthiness and of the need for discipline. These things concern the Buried Life, the man's innermost being. In troubling over them he arrives at his most real self, which is at least morally rational. Thus our Lord looked past the most reckless conduct of a man's life, finding within the unworthy a soul of worthiness, the true human life with which profligacy is essentially incongruous.

That I do not overstrain a mere phrase in this interpretation may be seen first by the fact referred to in my previous paper on the Apologia of Jesus, in which it appeared that this parable, like the two others linked with it, was suggested by the actual drawing near to Him of crowds of moral outcasts in response to His proclamation, not of mercy, but of a high and severe ideal of discipleship. And again the interpretation is illustrated by His prayer for His enemies. Apparently it was while He was being nailed to the Cross that Jesus prayed, *Father, forgive them; for they know not what they do*. The imperfect

tense introducing the prayer suggests that the
words were repeated with every blow of the
hammer upon His hands and feet. And the plea
He advanced was that His enemies had no idea
how much pain they were causing Him. The
implication of the plea was that if they had
known they would not have inflicted it. His
penetrative searching of men's hearts led Him
to despair of no man, and to the very last Jesus
refused to believe that the innermost heart of
anyone could be hopelessly cruel.

It is a further confirmation of this view of
His confidence in man's interior life that, in
His comment upon the parable of the unrighteous steward, He declared, *If therefore ye
have not been faithful in the unrighteous mammon,
who will commit to your trust the true riches? And
if ye have not been faithful in that which is another's,
who will give you that which is your own?* The true
riches, which, as ever in His teaching, are
spiritual treasures, are here set over against
money and visible possessions, and, by the old
Hebrew poetic parallelism, it is suggested that
these invisible riches, the only real wealth, are
by their nature our own, even when not in our
actual possession.

Thus, through differently conditioned utter-

ances our Lord allows us to see something of
the unity of His mind. We follow the penetration
of His eye through outward circumstance to
inward life. Informed by His method of seeing
we come to realise, not indeed that the outward
being is a worthless shell, heterogeneous from
the kernel it contains, but that the shell is
shaped from within, and that, despite all vitia-
tion, the formative thing is the inward. We learn
that it is spirit which supremely counts. And
we are encouraged to believe that if we will be
true to what we know, we shall find increasingly
that the innermost thing of all is indeed good
and that, as S. Chrysostom so nobly said, the
true Shekinah is the soul of man.

If we will be true to ourselves—this brings
me to see in the mind of Jesus His emphasis
upon Consistency, or the holding together of
the various parts of man's entire life. It is
obvious one may set store upon inward things
and yet achieve no consistency of character.
The deepest in me may be good, my soul may
be, as in the language of the psalmists, *my glory*,
and yet my total life may be a miscellany. The
incense from the most Holy court of the Temple
may be sweet and yet scarce transmit its

fragrance even to the Holy place, while in the outer courts there may be a shameless traffic. Where such is the case even the long-suffering of God, and the original grandeur of His work in us may become exhausted, and the central decay set in so that over the portals of the soul may be written at last, Ichabod: the glory has departed.

Now, despite all that is unsatisfactory in the generally received ideas as to our Lord's character, the world has certainly learnt from Him such a hatred of religious play-acting as is the beginning of Consistency. The elementary teachings here, as in the case of the principle of inwardness, are broadly accepted. For all time the hypocrite has been stigmatized appropriately in such phrases as those about the posturing in public during the occasions of prayer, and again in the exposure of the sham of Corban, and in the magnificent, hateless invective of the xxiiird chapter of S. Matthew.

On the other hand, how emphatic He was in proclaiming His commands over us for positive well-doing. *Not every one that saith unto Me, Lord, Lord, shall enter into the Kingdom of Heaven; but he that doeth the will of My Father which is in heaven....If ye know these things, blessed are ye if ye do them.*

But the same mind which gave us these sayings offered us also a guidance, springing from experience, as to the way of obedience to what is good. If the inward is the formative, He seems to say, then it is urgent that we should be careful to give it the sovereignty of administration. And what Jesus taught upon this matter He Himself first achieved. Thus, when He was accused of casting out demons by the aid of demons, He shewed the impossibility of an effective and yet self-divided life. There can be no question that in what He said upon this theme we have a fragment of autobiography. He was looking back to the Wilderness-conflict preceding His ministry. And the activity of His works He ascribed to the fact of the inner consistency consequent upon that struggle. He was not self-divided. He had won the decisive victory of life. He had bound the strong man and hence was able to conquer the strong man's servants. It is such an inner consistency, the ethical supremacy of a unified soul, which always accounts for the energy of the best people. The younger Pliny, by natural gift and training a shrewd observer of men, remarks in one of his letters, in illustration of a passage in Thucydides,

that there is less force of character in good
people than in bad. This may be an exag-
geration, but it represents a truth. Cicero came
near to the secret of the matter, when he said
to his friend Atticus that Pompey always won
in a bad cause and failed in the best of causes,
adding that in the one case he knew—what was
not difficult to know—how to act, and in the
other did not know. For it may be freely admitted that evil is commonly quicker in action
than good, and, as Ruskin has somewhere said,
while medicine often fails of its effect poison
never fails. So it is that things are often more
ready to the hand of the evil man and the evil
cause than adapted for the use of the right-
minded and the just, and the supreme need of
the good is that they should make sure of the
base of their action; in the word of Jesus, that
they should not attempt, as too readily they do,
to spoil the strong man before they have bound
him. Accordingly Jesus not only denounced the
duplicity of the hypocrite, He appealed also for
those decisions of the will by which a man's
inner and secret life wins control over his entire
existence. At different times and to different
persons He urged the same plea for the attainment of an undivided mind. *No man can serve two*

masters: for either he will hate the one, and love the other; or else he will hold to one, and despise the other. Ye cannot serve God and mammon....No man, having put his hand to the plough, and looking back, is fit for the Kingdom of God.

There is a passage in the Fourth Gospel which gathers up these sayings upon Consistency. *The wind bloweth where it listeth....so is everyone that is born of the Spirit.* It has been a misfortune that this word of Jesus has so often been applied to the determinations of the Holy Ghost, for the comparison does not lie between the wind and the Spirit, but between the wind and the regenerate soul. It is the soul that moves, where it chooses to move, that cries, like Browning's Paracelsus,

I see my way as birds their trackless way.
I shall arrive.

The soul that has received the wisdom of Jesus and the indwelling of the Spirit is unified, autonomous, sovereign. And in this it conforms to its great type, the Lord Himself, whose whole witness before men was offered in *the power of an indissoluble life.* When in the last conversations before the Passion, having declared to the Eleven, *Whither I go, ye know the Way,* He was challenged by Thomas with the words, *Lord,*

*we know not whither Thou goest; how know we
the way?* Jesus answered, *I am the Way* ('Εγώ
εἰμι ἡ ὁδὸς), *and the Truth, and the Life: no one
cometh unto the Father, but by Me.* The answer,
like all His answers to men's questions, went
beyond but did not ignore the point which had
been raised. That point concerned in the first
place His own immediate future, not that of
His questioner. And to this the reply was that
the Way He went was intimately related to
Himself. In a deeper sense than the Psalmist
used the words, in His heart were the high-
ways to Zion. There was a kinship between
His outward experience and His inward dis-
tinctiveness. He was the law of His own development, the path of His own advance. That
Providence, which in our case has to unify the
heterogeneousness of Life, converting all acci-
dents to good, and moulding our environment
into a shield for the nascent spirit, was in His
case rendered needless by His own simple
acceptance of all the outward events of His life,
as ministrants to spirituality, an acceptance
possible and accomplished through the un-
warped sovereignty of His will. It may be
added that in this declaration, I am my own
way, we can see how truly, as our archetype,

He met the necessities of Thomas, who craved
outward guidance—a voice, a body to see and
to touch—since for him, as for us all, the
perfection of being could only be attained by a
new birth into the realm of the Spirit.

The inwardness of Jesus thus unfolds through
an outwardness into a final unity of being. The
insistence upon inner cohesion is matched by
reiteration of the need for outer expression, and
this not simply in the interests of practical
morality, but in the larger interests of the whole
life, thought and feeling no less than the will
to do.

I see next that the animating principle of His
mind, and so the shaping power of all His
teaching, was His Vision of God.

To Jesus, as we know from an explicit
utterance, the fundamental doctrine of Revelation was the Divine Unity. *Hear, O Israel; the
Lord our God, the Lord is one; and thou shalt love
the Lord thy God with all thy heart, and with all
thy soul, and with all thy mind, and with all thy
strength. This is the great and first commandment.*
That is to say, man must gather up all his
powers in one great unity of loving, he must be
at one with himself in loving God, because God

is at one in Himself. A belief in the Unity of
God lay at the foundation of all the workings of
our Lord's mind.

But He did not theorise about God. He
beheld God. And the vision was not that brief
glimpse through broken clouds which sometimes
is mine. It was close and diurnal.

A Jewish Rabbi once wrote, " God is near
in every kind of nearness." Whether the saying
owes anything to the New Testament or not,
it aptly sums up the religiousness of the teaching of Jesus. In the minds of many Orientals
of His day, the monarchical conception of God
removed Him to a distance from His world, and
deputed to angels the administration of Nature.
With our Lord it was otherwise. For Him God
was ever present as a perceived glory of love
and wisdom. In this perception lay the prophetic distinction of Jesus. He moved as a
sighted person amongst the blind—the blind
who yet, as He deemed, should have been able
to see, so that He was surprised, it is said, at
men's unbelief. In contrast to our faint and
occasional seeing, His vision of God recalls that
famous dream De Quincey has given us from
Richter, the dream of one who thought himself carried through the skies by a heavenly at-

tendant, past innumerable star-systems, through depths of inter-stellar blackness, until, appalled by the all-engulfing night, he cried aloud in distress. Thereupon, said the dreamer, the Form by his side that carried him, touched his eyes as with the flowing of a breath, and the Universe was lit up before him, and he saw that nowhere was there any dark at all, but a sea of light, upon which the suns floated as ash-grey blossoms. Such a sea broke everywhere for Jesus—upon hillside and lake, upon all sentient life and around all human souls. It was the Divine love that shaped and nourished and sought to make all things glad. The Father clothed the grass of the field with lilies, fed the sparrow, and suffered in its fall. He whispered His secrets to babes. He met the soul in its secret oratory. His kingdom came upon men in the vanishing of their sicknesses and in the expulsion of their recalcitrancies. He indwelt the hearts of humble men, so that when they spoke of Him, despite their rudest accent, it was not they that spoke but the Spirit of their Father speaking in them. The nearness of God became at last, when the soul surrendered to it, an interpenetration of the Human and the Divine, a sublimation of that roadside scene on the way to Jericho, where two men, though alien to each other in blood and tradition, became one in a sacrament of brotherhood.

This Vision of the Presence moulded the several teachings of Jesus as in His treatment of the Sabbath-question and of the questions of ritual and of prayer. The nearness of God in every kind of nearness required only that one, just where he was, should lean back upon Him, to ask and receive all that it is fitting a man should know, even as the beloved disciple leaned back upon the Master's breast at the Last Supper. So for those who were loyal to Jesus problems of method in worship received the principle of their solution, and that men ought always to pray and not to faint became a counsel of possibility, because it called for neither shrine, nor posture, nor word, as essential concomitant of devotion.

Was it not also as moved by an awareness of the Presence of God that Jesus so magnified His Grace? God as good could not be so near sinful men without either saving or destroying. And that the Presence was not, at least as yet, a Presence of doom was evidenced by all the creative energies put forth in Nature and in Providence. So those enfolding arms that sought to win men could never regulate their pressures of love as men fixed the wages of labour. As God caused His sun to shine upon the evil and the good the Divine Householder gave to the last coming of His workers as to the first, His eye being kindly.

All these varied teachings concerning God and the religious life cohere. Whether the theme be what we call Nature, or Providence, or the Inspiration of disciples, or Worship, or Grace, the God with whom we have to do is with us in the immediacy of Love. This was the stedfast perception of Jesus. The unity of His teachings proceeded from the fact that His mind was of one texture throughout, an unforced and living thing, woven upon a loom set within the gateways of the stars. He saw continually that of which our mystical singers have occasional glimpses, as when Francis Thompson wrote,

For all the past, read true, is prophecy,
And all the firsts are hauntings of some Last,
And all the springs are flash-lights of one Spring.
Their leaf, and flower, and fall-less fruit
Shall hang together on the unyellowing bough;
And silence shall be music mute
For her surcharged heart. Hush thou!
These things are far too sure that thou shouldst
    dream
Thereof, lest they appear as things that seem.

In the last place in the Apocalyptic quality of the Mind of Jesus we have the synthesis of all its subordinate unities.

Jewish Apocalyptic arose, I know, out of a somewhat despairing sense of the failures of Politics and Religion. But Christian Apocalyptic springs from the invincible optimism of Jesus, as He faced an evil world bathed in the light of God. And, most surely, just as Science seeks the secret connection of man's visible body with his invisible mind, so every vital religion has, or seeks, an apocalypse. Apocalyptic is the vindication and achievement of those whose faith has been tested, approved, perfected. It is the Divine moment when, in the language of Plotinus, the man who has attained to fellowship with God has himself the similitude of Him. For to have the similitude of God is to have the power of transcending earthly conditions. It is to see what is seen by God *of Whom, and through Whom and unto Whom are all things*. The picture may at first be terrible; for machinery which has proved obsolete must needs be thrown aside, and for those who have become obdurate to the pleadings of the Spirit some more drastic method is evidently necessary, and, in dealing with these, Apocalyptic is the answer of the

Spiritual Universe to the desecration of man. But afar off is an end to tears; *the former things are passed away.*

Now much of what our Lord said about the Last Things has been ignored by those to whom the inwardness of His religion is the ruling Christian principle. The feeling has been, I believe, that perhaps a lower thought-element crept into the memory of the Apostolic Church, tangling the quiet radiance of a lofty mind with the lightnings of popular theology. But so far as we have disparaged this side of the teaching preserved in the Gospels, we have failed to realise what that holy thing is which we call an inward thing, spirit. Our difficulties have been largely due to the dominance of imagery. We are driven to the use of "matter moulded forms of speech," and these too often import into our thinking about the soul something of the very inertness and bondage of material objects. Jewish Rabbinic theology was surely right when it taught that the nearness of God is determined by the conduct of man and by his realisation of this nearness, that is, by his knowledge of God, for this is a judgment which safeguards the moral character of God. The symbol of nearness however, like all symbols, is capable of misleading us. As against this error, apocalyptic religion insists that when we refuse God we are not simply left to ourselves. God is still in actual relation to the man who has refused Him. So also if, changing our metaphor, we speak of God as a sea of light around all human souls, yet let us remember it is God of Whom we speak, God as possessing in Himself all that begets in us the qualities of personal life. If we keep to our figure, then, at least, it is not a quiescent sea by which we are beset, but one that beats and breaks and may blind with myriad coruscation. Holding with Jesus that the regenerate soul is autonomous, moving as it listeth, we can concede no less mobility to Him Who begat it. While we believe that the One is the Good, we cannot conceive Him as being without variation of method. With every change in us there must be change in Him. So just because God's attitude considers ours, Man carries in himself the moment of Apocalypse. The skies break and the stars fall, thrones are set and books opened, when this pilgrim of the Universe, reaching the watershed of his life, chooses the path that winds to the right, or plunges downward.

Such a point of decision, wherein Man reacts

upon God, was reached by our Lord and by His judges, in His Passion. And there is no more cogent illustration of the Unity of His Mind than His great saying to them, *Henceforth shall the Son of Man be seated at the right hand of the power of God*, as S. Luke records the words, or, *Henceforth ye shall see the Son of Man sitting at the right hand of power, and coming on the clouds of heaven*, as S. Matthew has them. Now, unhappily the Authorised version has misled many generations of English Christians by rendering the time note in both these verses, *Hereafter* instead of *Henceforth*. That arose from the intrusion of dogma upon exegesis. The real meaning is very clear to anyone who consults the Greek in both places and then compares both, but especially Luke's phrase, with the use in documents of New Testament times, as Professor Deissmann has shewn us in his *Bible Studies* (p. 253). Unquestionably we should read, *Henceforth*, not the vague *Hereafter*. What our Lord said expressed His own assured conviction that from the very moment of His humiliation and death He would come with power, in an ever-continuing, ever-growing Advent, as come on a clear spring day vast cumulus clouds throned upon each other in dazzling deeps of white above the outspread awestruck earth; He would come with growing majesty and undeniable strength, such as even a Sadducean priesthood would be compelled to admit.

It may be perfectly true that Jewish Apocalyptists and even S. Paul, using similar language, might mean something a good deal more material than this, but we shall greatly err if we refuse to credit our Lord with any originality of mind. Every study of His methods as a teacher, especially of His use of metaphor and parable, shews Him as employing language that is capable of differently graded spiritual interpretations, the profoundest of which must be the most intimate to His mind. Certainly whatever use He made of the mental machinery of His time was His own, and we commit a very big mistake when we force His apocalyptic speech into the mould of Daniel or of Enoch, or even of the Epistles to the Thessalonians, however true it may be that (if we may vary the imagery) from those who went before Him He gathered seed-thoughts, and to those who followed bestowed germinal fruits of His own Mind.

There is no need that we should reject as too modern this conception of our Lord's Return with power from the moment of His death. For while the Jewish people of His time lived in constant expectation of a literal and bodily return of Elijah, Jesus Himself shewed how easily He could employ in a higher sense the language of Return, spiritualising it in a very free way, by claiming that Elijah had indeed returned in the person of John the Baptist. This certainly affords us no complete parallel to the language He used later about His own Return, but it is striking evidence of the freedom with which He could change into imagery the very literal beliefs of His day. A closer parallel may be found in one of the letters of Cicero, in which reference is made to the posthumous influence of Caesar, under this very same imagery. " If things go on thus," he writes, "I like not the Ides of March. For he should never have come back, nor fear compelled us to ratify his acts; or else—heaven's curse light upon him dead though he be—so high was I in his favour that, seeing the Master is slain and we are not free, he was a Master not to be rejected at my time of life. I blush, believe me; but I have written, and will not blot it out"[1]. Language like this might have been employed by Caiaphas

[1] *Letters to Atticus*, xv. 4.

in relation to Jesus, during those years in which
the Church was so steadily gathering adherents
that even *a great company of the priests became
obedient to the faith;* only that the Jew, more
deeply sinning than the Roman, in place of a
fearful acceptance of the acts of Jesus, embarked
upon ever more desperate courses of opposition.
The two men, Cicero and Caiaphas, were at
one in this, that each was forced to see a hated
Master come back with power in the events that
followed his seeming overthrow. Caesar came
back in the acts of the Government that suc-
ceeded him, and in that personal ascendancy
of the hero as ruler which for centuries was
to direct the life of the Roman people.
Jesus came back, as He declared He would,
in the tremendous spiritual urge that swept
like a tide through the world, winning for the
Kingdom of God a multitude no man could
number, and marking out in reprobation, as
by an angel's dividing hand, those who confirmed their rejection of Him by their persecu-
tion of His Church. Again the parallel is not
perfect, for the event was unique, and the
presence of Jesus in the Church and the World
was vastly more than the presence of Caesar in
the Empire of Augustus, but the illustration

points the direction in which the Return-Teaching of Jesus must be read.

Nor does this interpretation of the Return equate merely a spiritual personal impulse of unusual power. It was, veritably, an outward Return, seeing that it involved institutional separations and movements within the Churches, which He thereby gathered together—separations from the outworn Jewish economy, movements of the redeemed communities into the organic oneness of a world-wide Church—whereby their life glowed with new power, the grace hitherto operating in some isolation, now most truly being *multiplied through the many;* while on the other hand, the Judgment He inflicted, the darkening of a reprobated people, with all the weakness in practical effort and slackening footstep such a loss of vision involves—Judgment which haply might turn the mind again to God—this we may trace in those words of 2 Baruch, which were written after the fall of Jerusalem:

For the youth of the world is past,
And the strength of the creation already
  exhausted,
And the advent of the times is very short,
Yea, they have passed by;
And the pitcher is near to the cistern,
And the ship to the port,

> And the course of the journey to the city,
> And life to its consummation[1].

The Apocalyptic of Jesus thus construed was the natural development of His earlier teaching. It rested upon His intense realisation of spiritual life—life which was first of all, for men, inward and at times buried, but which persisted through all the sin and failure of daily walk and conversation, life which as a real good was insuppressible, and which it was the purpose of God to unfold in an outward as well as an inward consistency. Even the judgment of reprobation in the Return was not without its aspect of hope, arising from this sense of good. *Ye shall not see Me henceforth*, He cried to the guilty city a day or two before He suffered, *till ye shall say, Blessed is He that cometh in the Name of the Lord*[2].

Above all it was His consciousness of God, His quiet assurance of the Father's Presence, not remote in some heavenly court, but entering however faintly into all earthly things, clothing field and bird and man, and indwelling the learner's soul—it was this utter awareness and open vision of God which led Jesus to use the

---

[1] 2 Baruch LXXXV. 10; in Dr Charles' *Apocrypha and Pseudepigrapha*, II. 479.

[2] I follow Matthew's placing of these words (xxiii. 39).

language of Apocalyptic, as denoting God's final mastering of things, the flooding up of Deity through all the intercourse of men.

And we, reading our Lord's words in their immediate references to the time in which He stood and the people He came to save, are strengthened to see later fulfilments of His teaching also, in cycles of historic crisis, in those periodic religious quickenings which the Church has from time to time experienced, and to anticipate some Last Advent when God shall become all in all.

There was no schism in the mind of Jesus. His Apocalyptic was the crowning assertion that Religion claimed the whole of life; it was the insistence that body and even that extension of man's physical life—the visible order in which he moves and toils—are both included in the domain of spirit, that Life ultimately is one, and that for every man, no less than for Jesus Himself, mind and flesh, heaven and earth, should be as the seamless robe woven from the top throughout.

IX

HIS CUP

OUR Lord spoke of His Cup some three or four times. The chief occasions are recorded in S. Mark x. 32–40, xiv. 23–24, xiv. 32–36.

In the first we have His reply to the request of James and John for high places in His Kingdom. *Ye know not what ye ask. Are ye able to drink the cup that I drink? or to be baptized with the baptism that I am baptized with? And they said unto Him, We are able. And Jesus said unto them, The Cup that I drink ye shall drink; and with the baptism that I am baptized withal shall ye be baptized: but to sit on my right hand, or on my left hand is not mine to give: but it is for them for whom it hath been prepared.* Two things about the Cup appear here. It was a Cup of tremendous contents, difficult for anyone to drink. And yet it was finally announced, James and John should actually drink of it. A third point is inferred— the reference was to the coming Passion. That is involved in both metaphors—the Cup and the baptism. At another time the Lord said, in a context pregnant with storm, *I have a baptism to be baptized with; and how am I straitened till it be accomplished!* Cup and baptism both declare the Passion. The Cup which He had to drink, the baptism when all God's waves and billows should go over Him—these, then, in an experience of suffering James and John were to share with Him.

Did they indeed drink His Cup? I suppose the usual reply is to point to the early death of James as recorded in The Acts, and to the exile of John at Patmos as supposed from The Apocalypse. But was there anything here so surpassingly difficult for men who had been told over and over again that they *must* take up the Cross and follow Jesus? So far from denying their ability to suffer for His sake, that was the very thing which He had repeatedly declared every disciple must be willing to do. And that certainly they did achieve, and this not without the addition of infinite blessing. A flash of the sword and one of the Sons of Thunder leaped into the Glory of Paradise; while John's bare island home at Patmos (if banishment indeed was his lot) became a theatre of vision and of victory. Since those days thousands have taken the Cup of Martyrdom and found it not difficult to drink, not bitter but exceedingly sweet.

Further, the Cup of Jesus was certainly more than physical pain. He did not shrink from the nails of the Cross. He refused the stupefying potion offered Him when He hung there. As Browning expressed it in *Prospice*, He would not let Death bandage His eyes and bid Him creep past the post of the foe. Nor was it merely physical decease from which He so shrank. The actual end was full of peace. *Father*, He was heard to say, *into Thy hands I commend my Spirit.* It must have been in some other than a physical quality that His Cup was so terrible.

I come to S. Mark's second reference. It is in the narrative of the Last Supper. *And He took a Cup, and when He had given thanks, He gave to them: and they all drank of it.* This does not speak in so many words of the Cup as being His, but when He gave it He said, *This is My blood of the covenant, which is shed for many;* S. Matthew adds, *unto remission of Sins.* So James and John drank the Lord's Cup symbolically at least at that Supper before He suffered. Was that all? Surely no, He could scarcely have questioned their ability to participate, even after the spiritual manner S. Paul demanded of the Corinthians, in the ritual acts of the Holy Eucharist. Yet the reference is important because it indicates the nature of that ultimate experience of which the ritual drinking was symbolic. It was an experience connected with the remission of Sins. This is a signpost to me.

I turn to S. Mark's third reference. *And they come unto a place which was named Gethsemane: and He saith unto His disciples, Sit ye here, while I pray. And He taketh with Him Peter and James and John, and began to be greatly amazed, and sore troubled.* Each of these three men had undertaken to share His Passion: James and John, as we have seen in their confident word, *We are able*: Peter, when He declared, *If I must die with Thee, I will not deny Thee.* Therefore Jesus called them to join His vigil, and they saw His agony and heard some of His pleading. *He saith unto them, My Soul is exceeding sorrowful even unto death: abide ye here, and watch. And He went forward a little, and fell on the ground, and prayed that, if it were possible, the hour might pass away from Him. And He said, Abba, Father, all things are possible unto Thee; remove this Cup from Me: howbeit not what I will, but what Thou wilt.* So the Cup of which, as He had said, James and John were to partake was a cup from which for a time He Himself recoiled. No wonder He had doubted their ability to drink it. Yet the fact remains that finally He said,

The Cup that I drink ye shall drink. We have seen
that His Cup was more than a cup of physical
anguish. What spiritual element did it contain?

Now, in any question of New Testament interpretation it is a wise rule to trace out the
related Old Testament usages. What, then, does
the Cup stand for in the Old Testament? We
find that taking only those occurrences in which
the meaning is figurative, there are 19 passages
to be considered. Of these, three only are
places signifying blessing. In a fourth instance
the Cup is one of sinful pleasure. In all the
15 other cases the Cup is that of *the wrath of God.*
You have it so in Isaiah, Jeremiah, Ezekiel,
Zechariah and The Psalms. In all these passages
the meaning is terrible. In one of them it is
appalling with a vividness which reminds me of
some of the most frightful battle-pictures in
Homer. It is the word of the Lord through
Ezekiel to the people of Judah, comparing
Judah's doom with that of the sister-kingdom
of Israel. *Thou shalt drink of thy sister's cup, which
is deep and large: thou shalt be laughed to scorn and
had in derision; it containeth much. . . . Thou shalt even
drink it and drain it out, and thou shalt gnaw the
sherds thereof, and shalt tear thy breasts: for I have
spoken it, saith the Lord God* (Ezek. xxiii. 32 ff.).

Now nothing but some very great horror could have forced the pathetic cries of Gethsemane from the strong Son of God, Who already had faced a violent death many times. I am compelled to feel it must have been this Cup of which the Old Testament so often speaks that Jesus had to drink. This is the symbol chosen by Him wherewith to describe His woe, the Cup of the Wrath of God, which the ungodly at the last are forced to drink and to drain, gnawing the very sherds of the vessel, while with one clutching hand they tear at their agonised breasts amid the clattering laughter of Hell. This is that concerning which the Lord prayed: *Father, all things are possible unto Thee; remove this Cup from Me: howbeit not what I will, but what Thou wilt.*

I understand by the Wrath of God not the mere hot displeasure of a magnified man. I believe God to be personal, but His Personality is in the scale of forces that shape and control all human life, forces that are world-wide in scope. When we speak of God, we speak of Him *of Whom, and through Whom and unto Whom are all things*. The wrath of God is an inward experience. It is the reaction of the Divine in us against our sins. If I turn to literature for an illustration, the story of Arthur Dimmesdale in *The Scarlet Letter* is the purest exhibition of this reaction known to me. "'Hester,' said he, 'hast thou found peace?' She smiled drearily, looking down upon her bosom. 'Hast thou?' she asked. 'None! nothing but despair!' he answered. 'What else could I look for, being what I am, and leading such a life as mine? Were I an atheist—a man devoid of conscience —a wretch with coarse and brutal instincts—I might have found peace long ere now. Nay, I never should have lost it! But, as matters stand with my soul, whatever of good capacity there originally was in me, all of God's gifts that were the choicest have become the ministers of spiritual torment. Hester, I am most miserable.'"

So also in the Old Testament the Wrath of God is the torment of sin consciousness. Immediately after the words of Ezekiel concerning the Cup, follow these: *Therefore thus saith the Lord God: Because thou hast forgotten Me, and cast Me behind thy back, therefore bear thou also thy lewdness and thy whoredoms.* We drink the cup of the fury of the Lord when, having ignored Him and rejected His grace—though it be carelessly and inadvertently—we feel at last returning upon our power to will, and all our native instincts of good, and all our experience of something high, a full sense of our sins as our very own. Then is our consciousness like that of Peter after his denial, or even like that of Judas declaring *I have betrayed innocent blood*. It is the sense of guilt, of an evil done by this hand, this tongue, this very self—something that has now become a part of me, an inner degradation making hell within and all about my path.

But the Old Testament taught also that a man need never drink this cup alone, nor indeed need he ever taste its bitterest dregs. There is in the prophets a passionate outcrying of God to His People in language such as this, *How shall I give thee up, Ephraim? How shall I deliver thee, Israel? . . . Mine heart is turned within Me, My compassions are kindled together*. And in Isaiah we read more than that: *Thou hast made Me to serve with thy sins, Thou hast wearied Me with thine iniquities*. God made to serve with my sins! God made my accomplice! As though Francis Thompson's *Any Saint* might be Any sinner too:

> When thou to thee pluck'st down,
> Strong clod!
> The neck of God.

And Ezekiel again has this most penetrating vision of moral things: *And they that escape of you shall remember Me among the nations whither they shall be carried captives, how that I have been broken with their whorish heart.* So the dark shadow of Gethsemane is adumbrated in the Old Testament, and light that has arisen out of Calvary's thick gloom had its foreshining in the prophets. The Cup of wrath God Himself drinks with guilty men. And forgiveness is wrought out for us by One who is Himself oppressed and broken by what He forgives. *I, even I, am He that blotteth out thy transgressions for Mine own sake.*

With these sayings in mind I return to the interpretation of that Cup which James and John were to share. I see that Jesus shrank from His Cup, and that in drinking of it at last the Lord was undergoing in some very deep sense a consciousness of sin. But I cannot think this was sin as abstractly or theologically considered. All the habitual working of His mind was unphilosophic, concrete and poetic. Surely what He bore was first of all quite inevitably the very sin which He saw being done, or about to be done, and with which in no mysterious but in a very natural manner His own steps were involved.

Two simple illustrations will make this connexion clear. The first is from the Old Testament story of Moses. When Moses was sent to effect the liberation of the Hebrew race, his first efforts ended in disastrous failure. His very mission increased the suffering of the slaves. They had thenceforth to find their own materials in the brickmaking and to work harder than ever. And this was because Moses had interfered. Accordingly he prayed: *Lord, wherefore hast Thou evil entreated this people? Why is it Thou hast sent me?* My second illustration is from modern missionary literature. The chief sorrow of David Livingstone's last years in Africa was his experience of the overwhelming and circumventing power of evil. He found that, instead of missionaries labouring in his track, those who tried to do so broke down and died, while the slave-dealers, whom he had hoped so utterly to defeat, profited by his discoveries and utilised the very roads into the interior, which he had opened up for the purpose of redeeming the whole country from bondage of every kind. Thus the evil the pioneer went out to overthrow was increased at first in its extent and character by his efforts, and he was forced to recognise its triumph as coming through himself.

These illustrations may suggest to us some idea of the tormenting sorrow in which our Lord brought His work to a close. The Agony was the apprehension of a rising tide of sin all about Him, of sin as occasioned by Himself. His very mission to save was provoking greater ruin. Every step He took forward quickened temptation in evil men. He had sometimes healed on the Sabbath day. How thankful I am that He did! We have needed all the large liberality of thought revealed in such actions as these to maintain—and scarcely have we done that—a reasonable view of the Sunday question. But that Divine generosity He shewed, so far as the Jewish religionists were concerned, served only to evoke intenser prejudices and a more blinding hate. So His whole witness to truth worked like a provocation. It was so from the first gracious beginnings in Galilee. And at the last He uttered that saddest of all His sayings, *If I had not come and spoken unto them, they had not had sin.* What a frightful thought—for Him! It involved Him in their sin. And this was no mere fleeting illusion bred of despondency. It was a working of His mind, whereby was brought home to Him the truth of that solidarity of Life which binds the righteous to the wicked, and which makes it impossible, unless God would disrupt the world, to separate the saint from the dooms of his fellow-men.

Thus it was with Him: at the end sin reached its most hideous height. The waters of a full cup were wrung out to Him. And to His most intimate consciousness, through Judas in his kissing, through Peter's denials, through Caiaphas rending his robes, through Pilate washing his hands, through priests and mob in their execrations, sin came in upon Him as His own, and looming through every vile action in the tragedy was a revelation of human nature at its vilest—the sin of the world. The cup was deep and large. And it was said to Him, said by those forces and laws in our common human life which are the hands of the Living God, *Thou shalt even drink it and drain it out, and thou shalt gnaw the sherds thereof.*

In this experience of sin there must have lain all those tortures of misgivings concerning moral things which come to the best of men in moments of outward defeat and physical strain —moral misgiving that would lead on naturally to the darkest climax of all, the feeling of dereliction. Hence that cry from the Cross, the bitterness of which lies partly in the fact that it is a question, *My God, My God, why hast Thou forsaken Me?* The light was fading out from a soul that never before had known, but only sometimes shudderingly imagined, the outer darkness. It was fading out because, as we have seen, the facts of Life actually were that sin at its worst was occasioned by His own actions. It would have been of no avail for any to have tried to comfort Him by declaring that the sin was first of all in the hearts of His enemies, because a sin that passes from conception to transgression ever grows in the process. So it was that at this point Jesus inevitably seemed to Himself to stand on one side with sinful men, as over against that other side, which now had become dread to Him—the Holy God.

Nevertheless under the guidance of the Spirit of Truth, Who, as Jesus in happier moments had promised, was to come to explain to us these mysterious happenings, we are permitted to see what the Lord Himself in His hours of deepest Passion could not see, namely that just when He seemed to be responsible for men's sins, and to be removed an infinite distance from God, He was manifesting that Passion of the Eternal of which the prophets had spoken, and not only manifesting it, but carrying it to its point of complete penetration; for the Incarnation is more than a revelation of what God eternally is: it is an achievement by God. And the words of ancient revelation, *Thou hast made Me to serve with thy sins...I have been broken with their whorish heart,* merge into the great saying of the Apostle Paul, *God was in Christ,* Christ Crucified, *reconciling the World unto Himself.*

This brings me to see the Cup of Jesus with a light falling upon it. It becomes now

> the Holy Cup
> With all its wreathen steps of passion-flowers
> And quivering sparkles of the ruby stars,

a thing of beauty. It is lifted to the lips of Jesus and not to His alone, but to the lips of James and John and, each according to His measure, to the lips of all holy Souls too. Any saint, sings Thompson, is

> Great arm-fellow of God!
> To the ancestral clod
> > Kin,
> And to cherubin;
> Bread predilectedly
> O' the worm and Deity.

When we ask, What is that measure of soul
in which our portion is meted out to us, we find
the answer mostly in one word—Love. There is
that unevadable sharing of things which, as we
have seen, comes from our human solidarity. But
far more penetrating for commonalty is Love.
"The more a man loves," says Amiel, "the
more he suffers. The sum of possible grief for
each soul is in proportion to its degree of perfection." For through Love we not only read
each other's lives: we interpenetrate: we find
ourselves linked to and implicated with qualities,
moral and immoral, not of our own choosing.
Love confirms and deepens the natural lines of
our human oneness. It is, therefore, to human
life rather than to animal life we turn for interpretation of atonement. Family histories are
here of more value than all the myriad sacrifices
of Solomon. The truest types and foreshadowings
of the Cross lie not so much in Israel's ritual of
sacrifice, which was indigenous to the Semitic
mind but is exotic to the mind of the West, as
in her own actual sorrows and in things which
belong to the heart of all mankind. The true
loci classici of the Old Testament teaching concerning atonement are in such words as the cry
of David, *O my son Absalom, my son, my son*

Absalom! would God I had died for thee, O Absalom, my son, my son! or in the story of Hosea's desolate home.

Our English Revisers have in the margin of Proverbs xvi. 6 a very luminous saying: *By mercy and truth iniquity is atoned for.* The Cup of Jesus was mixed with these two: *mercy* (*khesedh, lovingkindness,* as it is often rendered, *leal-love* as Sir George Adam Smith translates) the intuitive and loyal sympathy whereby He felt Himself in all human souls: *truth* (*emeth*) the firmness and faithfulness to what is right in which a man cleaves after God. Perfect love is the blending of one soul with another. If a man really loved his neighbour as himself he would feel his neighbour's sins as his own. And if a man really loved God, with all his mind and soul and strength, he would share the Divine hatred of injustice, selfishness and untruth. In the coexistence of these two loves there must ever be pain. And as far as we cherish them so far do we taste what later was tasted by those zealous Apostles to whom the Lord said, when reconsidering their future growth in the light of His grace, *The Cup that I drink ye shall drink.* By this same grace we also may become administrators of that sacred

Passion by which the world is atoned to God.

Administrators of the Passion—such are the Lord's people to be: administrators not creators. For all that we can do is of His grace; and we do not achieve the atoning attitude; we receive it. The Passion of Christ as the final reaction of the Divine in human life against sin, because it was an event, remains unique. And it is manifestly supreme in purity and therefore in poignancy. How little can I mourn for my neighbour's sins, who sin so much myself! None of us ever comes very near the deep sorrow of Jesus, because we ourselves are so often selfish and untrue. We share His experience up to a point and then, like the Three in the Garden, we fall asleep! David weeping for Absalom does but foreshadow Christ. The kingly tears that were shed in the chamber over the city gate cannot compare for crystal-clearness with those that fell in Gethsemane. But well does the old Greek poet[1] say of a sacrifice that meets Divine acceptance,

One soul, I deem, in meeting such a debt
May clear the countless, if the heart be pure.

And the Passion of Christ, once an event in time,

---

[1] Sophocles: *Oed. Col.* 498-9.

now a heavenly reality, streams upon me and through me, as I am joined to my Lord by faith. All that He once was He ever is. All that He is I may become, for *He that is joined to the Lord is one Spirit*. The dynamic of the Cross is the Christ who died and lives for evermore. In Him I grow towards Holiness. And—here is a great wonder too—in me He grows towards the World. Through all elect souls whom He indwells does the Saviour draw near to the unreconciled. It is not a doctrine nor a formula that redeems the sinful. We are never saved until we meet our Saviour. But we may meet Him in His priests, in James and John and in all those who belong to the Holy Society of Faith, of which Christ is Head and King.

X

HIS ASCENSION

ONE of my friends, once discussing with me our Lord's survival of death, summed up the subject by saying, "I can believe that in some way the risen Jesus communicated to His disciples assurances of His continued existence and of His enhanced power, but that the disciples saw and conversed with a resuscitated body, and, finally, that that body floated into the sky, and was lost to view amongst the clouds—this is grotesque." Such is, probably, the feeling of large numbers of thoughtful Christian people to-day, especially as regards the Ascension. To many, indeed, the story of the Ascension is just the final stage of a materialistic element present in the entire series of Resurrection-narratives, an element which, by at last becoming absurd, endangers the whole Easter message.

I have tried elsewhere—in *The Expositor*, November 1918—to examine as critically as I am able the value of the testimonies of the New Testament to the Risen and Ascended Lord. What I shall now set down will be taken in part from *The Expositor* article, but I shall not trouble the reader with any repetition of the criticism, and whoso desires to see what may be advanced in the way of historic evidence may be referred to the full essay. I will only say further, by way of introduction to this last study in the Life of our Lord, that, so far as the alleged grotesqueness of the Ascension is concerned, a spiritual aesthetic must certainly be one of the criteria of Truth, but S. Luke especially amongst the New Testament writers —and it is with him we have to do—ever presupposes in his readers a certain measure of imagination, and a certain quality of imagination. The alleged grotesqueness in the sacred narrative may be on the reader's part, just the gaucherie of a learned but over-drilled mind cut off somewhat from the renewing springs of its own deeper life.

He came one evening to the disciples, *the doors being shut for fear of the Jews,* and stood amongst them once more, as He had done on other occasions after His death. They all perceived Him and held converse with Him in some modes unfamiliar to us and new also to them. It is said *He opened their mind*—the group-

mind which hitherto had been latent enough
among their slightly jarring personalities. Some-
how He evoked a new spiritual attitude common
to them all. It was most evidently a spring of
joy that remained perennial after the Vision had
passed. Though we cannot know the method
of His opening action, it seems sure that it was
a priestly action, leading all these men to worship
with the angels and with the saints already
gathered to the Father in Heaven. In that hour
they became alive to things to which the prophets
had borne testimony, not as in the separateness
of a reasoned theological treatise written section
by section, but in the fulness of vision which
gathers up all our scattered glimpses of Truth
and Goodness and Beauty into one final Reality
—the Will of God. *He opened their mind that
they might understand the scriptures.* Afterwards,
it seemed as though He had taught them
this thing and that in so many words; for so
all our seminal visions branch out and yield
fruits we can count and weigh. But the Vision
itself—this was more than detailed instruction.
Yet I suppose in our commoner moods we covet
something more capable of tabulation or analysis
than ultimate truth. We are puzzled about the
Risen Lord. We should like to know how He

spoke and looked, and, perhaps, if we are not afraid of admitting the question, what clothes He wore.

Of course if we want to be absurd we shall read these narratives of vision as though they were a journalist's account of his interview with a famous person. But no speech with men from one who has crossed the Border can escape considerable subjective entanglements. Man never has that perfect knowledge about anything or anyone, of which Plotinus says that in it the perceiver attains to be what is perceived. The dress of any communicated idea is a dress the recipient himself provides. And most emphatically must this be the case in all supernormal experiences, such as intercourse with one who once was dead.

It is to Poetry we had better turn for aid in understanding anything so wonderful as this, because Poetry with its measures and balances is more akin to the undulating vital movements of the soul, than is the prose in which History is generally written. But first let a poet speak to us in prose of what he once saw and felt about Divine things. James Russell Lowell was in earnest discussion at the house of a friend. "As I was speaking," he afterwards reported, "the whole system rose up before me like a vague Destiny looming from the Abyss. I never before so clearly felt the Spirit of God in me and around me. The whole room seemed to me full of God. The air seemed to wave to and fro with the presence of something, I knew not what. I spoke with the calmness and clearness of a prophet." May I take that as a footnote to the lines in *The Cathedral*:

I, that still pray at morning and at eve,
Loving those roots that feed us from the past,
And prizing more than Plato things I learned
At that best academe, a mother's knee,
Thrice in my life perhaps have truly prayed,
Thrice, stirred below my conscious self have felt
That perfect disenthralment which is God.

In any case I prefer the poetry here to the prose. *That perfect disenthralment which is God—* is not that all that can be said? Or shall I put it in this word of Scripture, *Then opened He their mind*? It is a supernormal state, an unwalled consciousness. The lamps grow dim in the Upper Room and flicker out. The sounds from the streets die away. Only an owl hoots from the neighbouring thicket of Gethsemane beyond the city gates. But lights and darknesses, sounds and silences are nothing now to those Eleven men.

Earth breaks up, time drops away,
In flows heaven, with its new day
Of endless life, when He who trod,
Very Man and very God,
This Earth in weakness, shame and pain,
Dying the death whose signs remain
Up yonder on the accursed tree,—
Doth come again, no more to be
Of Captivity the thrall,
But the One God, All in All,
King of Kings, Lord of Lords,
As His servant John received the words,
"I died, and live for evermore[1]."

That—the perfect disenthralment—is something of what I mean about this Upper Room experience:

Earth breaks up, time drops away,
In flows heaven, with its new day.

Or again, it is Wordsworth who helps me, through his passionate commingling with God in the beauteous forms of Nature:

We are laid asleep
In body, and become a living soul:
While with an eye made quiet by the power
Of harmony, and the deep power of joy
We see into the life of things.

[1] Browning wrote (*Christmas Eve*, § x): "shall come again." I have ventured to use the present tense as more to my meaning and not I think unreasonably, for the lines in their original context are a very fine interpretation of the Roman celebration of the Mass.

The bodily life and the passing of time were nought, while the group-mind slowly opened under the breathings of the Heavenly Presence, that they might understand the Scriptures, that they might see into the life of things.

It was the last watch of the night. Already in the Temple the priests were preparing for the morning sacrifice, and watchers had mounted to the roof to look for the dawn breaking upon the walls of Hebron. Through the silent streets stole those Eleven disciples of the Lord, under a common impulse quickened by the joy of their night of vision. The bodily life had reacted at last against the stress of devotion. They wanted air and space and the hills through which to retain and absorb the vast visions of Redemption as He had shewn it to them. And under the constraint of the vision they went out to Olivet. *He led them out*, as some low-hanging star in the intense, jewelled sky had led the magi to His birthplace, *until they were over against Bethany.* Mists of the night were lying, like swathes of our long hayfield grasses, upon the hillsides, then, under the stirring of the first tremulous breaths of the onward rush of day, rising, and slowly rolling in ghostly waves. Still He led them on and higher, along a way they had often trodden before, until the ridge was reached when He turned and blessed them; and, as He turned, He was lifted up and slowly receded as upon some hitherto undiscovered path above the rock, wreathed in the yielding vapour. There was a gleam of feet whiter than mist and of hands outstretched in blessing, the sight of a visage once marred more than any man's, now majestic with the light of another world, a vision creating haunting glories in the mind, as when in the play Shakespeare's Leontes, seeing once more the eyes of his queen deemed long dead, exclaims with passion,

> Stars, stars,
> And all eyes else dead coals.

Then as the sun leaps up beyond the wall of Moab the clouds lift from the hills, the mist which half-veiled the Lord's rising form is rent into thin air, and He has passed. In vain may human eyes search the quickly clearing sky, but in the heart there is enshrined an image that can never perish, the source of that great note of joy wherewith the Gospel of S. Luke comes to a close.

146 ASPECTS OF THE WAY

It has often been remarked that there is no
record in the Gospels of any appearance of the
Risen Lord to unbelievers. This indicates at
once the subjective element in these narratives
to which I have already alluded. It remains for
me to do justice to the objective in them as well.
This was more than the basis of an intuition.
There was a message, but the message was incarnate, a presence, a form which challenged
the touch of hands. It was not, however, a
resuscitated body the disciples saw, but a body
builded out of that which had died, every
particle of which had been taken up and
spiritualised, as a plant takes up nitrates and
sulphates and phosphates from the soil around
it and converts them into protoplasm and
chlorophyll. It is spoken of as a body of *flesh
and bones*, yet clearly the flesh was not subject
to the same limitations as is our mortal body.
And here I recall the very striking support ac-
corded to Holy Scripture by some modern
scientists. "Each kind of organism," says
Professor J. A. Thomson, "has its own chemical
individuality....It looks as if a man is individual
not only to his finger-prints, but to his chemical
molecules. We come back to what was said of
old: 'All flesh is not the same flesh: but there

is one kind of flesh of men, another flesh of beasts, another of fishes, and another of birds[1].'"

This establishes the uniqueness of the bodily life of each of us, and it also suggests to us a point of departure for our thoughts about Life and Death, and especially for our thought of the Risen Christ.

If there is this bodily uniqueness in every one, how shall we conceive of the bodily life of Jesus? how shall we relate His physical frame to His normal consciousness? Now, no fact is more patent to us than the damaging effect of moral evil upon the structure of the body. Thus, the pursuit of certain trains of thought, such as enmity and lust, will set up pathological conditions in the body. Conversely, a life of goodwill, based upon joyous communion with God, helps our physical vigour. Can we not see the direction in which these facts point so far as they concern our Lord? We have no experience of the conscious life of one dwelling in unbroken communion with God. But such experience as we have, in our own alternating moods of good and evil, indicates something of the consequences to the whole life of a heavenly-mindedness, wherein the intellect is continually

[1] *Encyclo. of Religion and Ethics*, VIII. 2.

flooded with the love of God, and where the will is ever active in the service of man. Under such conditions would not the physical life be an index of the Spiritual, and correspond to the holiness of the inner state by some potentialities —if not indeed active powers—utterly unknown to sinful men like ourselves? Here may be the truth of the great stanza in Spenser's *Hymne in Honour of Beautie:*

> So every spirit, as it is most pure,
> And hath in it the more of heavenly light,
> So it the fairer bodie doth procure
> To habit in, and it more fairly dight
> With chearefull grace and amiable sight;
> For of the soule the bodie form doth take;
> For soule is forme, and doth the bodie make.

Such a physical life as was the Lord's before He suffered must certainly have offered possibilities of redemption from death which we, with our sin-soaked brain and spoiled nerve-tissue, cannot share, so that the actual mode of our resurrection may be necessarily different from His, though ultimately conforming to *the body of His glory.*

Further, we can see the fitness for the utilisation of the broken earthly body of Jesus in the creation of His heavenly body. It was

fitting so, not only because His holy will had
daily penetrated and suffused His flesh with its
own quality in motions which were veritable

Bright shoots of everlastingness,

but also because in Christ a new era of human
life was to be begun, and the new beginnings of
God are not revolutions but sublimations of the
Past. What this new beginning in the Resurrection and Ascension was has been finely expressed
by Bishop Chase in a lecture on *The Supernatural
Element in Our Lord's Earthly Life.* "If," he says,
"we believe in the Resurrection at all, we
believe in it as an event which is on a level with
creation itself—a reconciliation of the antithesis
of spirit and matter." In this reconciliation all
is conserved to man which belongs to his
propriety. The post-mortal condition is seen in
strict relation with his entire nature as both
body and spirit, while yet the Divine declaration runs, *Behold, I will do a new thing.*

The great truth which these artless Gospel
stories of the Risen and Ascending Lord convey,
but which those who first related them can have
scarcely measured, is the fact of the Risen Life
as, on the one hand, no ghostly thing, and on
the other, no physically limited thing, but a

spiritualisation of earthly elements, the efflor-
escence of the immanence of God, carrying with
it for loving and sorrowing beings assurances of
the continuity of our fellowship and of the
mobility and efficiency of our immortal life in
all the range of personal action. Such a truth,
with its implied sanctions for the culture of the
present order of our existence, and with its
hopes of joyous service and intercourse in that
order which is yet to come, appeals to every
heart that knows the love of God as being
a thing too congruous with all our richest
moments of experience to be doubted or with-
stood. We leap to it as to something which,
while beyond our power to have imagined, yet,
once declared to us, is seen to be characteristic
of God.

It is, of course, as participating in the general
aspects of the Risen life that the truth of the
Ascension is to be apprehended. The one glory
dies into the other, the light of moonset into the
majesty of sunrise. The credibility of the Ascension lies largely in this majesty; and one regrets
that the unimaginative mind which can see in
the narrative only a grotesque thing has been
of apiece with the conspicuous failure of Art to
produce a single picture helpful for the under-

standing of the event. It must be confessed, too, that the treatment of the subject by many commentators has been trivial in the extreme. We have greatly lacked an exposition of it couched in terms of moral dignity. Thus the Ascension has often been commended to our acceptance on certain commonplace grounds, such as the need of an indication to the Eleven of the close of the appearances of the Risen Lord. Doubtless, the event produced this effect. And certainly the entire epoch of manifestation was governed by that superintending wisdom of God which determines the many parts and fashions of revelation, adapting them to actually existing human needs. But we should dismiss from our minds all ideas of little purposes, and of self-regardfulness in One truly taken up into the central activity of God. Here was no piece of play-acting, such as Hebrew prophets had sometimes employed, but rather a life-development. In a certain loved garden of the South of England I have often watched at summer dusk the opening of the bloom of the evening primrose, as the loosening furls of petal, by pressure from within and by an outward invitation of shadow and dew, shook themselves free into expanded loveliness—the work of a few moments alone, although prepared for by all the plant's anterior life. With as little theatricality was that moment reached when the full glory of the Son of Man, as type of all our Race, wrought out the final separation from earthly conditions, and Manhood stood revealed as accomplished in the Divine. All that truly belonged to our personal life reached its destiny, the end for which through unnumbered ages the Spirit of God had worked at His chosen design. And, though we exclude that vulgarising of the event which would stage it for us, let us be careful to realise that the whole activity of the Lord was involved. We may learn here from the language concerning it in Scripture. The usage varies between two Greek words rendered *assumption* and *ascension*, and while the former is the more frequent as implying more the power of God upon the life He thus made more fully one with Himself, the latter carries with it the welcome thought of the co-operation of that life with His power. We cannot afford to neglect either term. *Taken up*—so the symbolic phrase runs—the Lord experienced the impact upon His perfected manhood of the Sovereign Will of the Universe. *Ascended*—again the word at its deepest is a figure of speech—He carried

with Him all that He had achieved in time of
the Wisdom of life.

For us who are to be younger brothers to this
Firstborn from the Dead and who may see the
apex of the truth of His Resurrection in the
story we have now considered, the Ascension
casts a beauty about the world beyond the hues
of sunshine, pointing the direction of the noblest
Art, and giving impulse to the Sciences that
concern the physical and moral welfare of men.
It teaches us,

> that a twofold world
> Must go to a perfect cosmos. Natural things
> And Spiritual,—who separates those two
> In art, in morals, or the Social drift,
> Tears up the bond of nature.

It opens to us a vision of the End for which
Man was made, when all things of sense and
time shall lie beneath his feet, when his earthly
home shall have been outgrown, and a new
earth and a new heaven be needed as his appropriate environment, and when, in entering
upon that higher state, he shall not so much
leave behind the lower, in which too often now
he seems imprisoned, as carry with him the
best it is able to contribute to the fulness of his
life. Thus the Ascension is the symbol of the

measure of man's life, of the gathering into himself of the very essence of his sense-conditioned activities. It is the pellucid spring of that joy which rises in the heart when our faith and hope are in God, for it shews us that the things which are to come, and which here we can but dimly discern, are yet not foreign to our nature, but infinitely friendly, at once surpassing imagination, and yet also of the very spirit to which we already belong.

EPILOGUE

THE WAY

DR JOHNSON, with that healthy objectivity which made him often an excellent spokesman of our British commonsense, once observed to Boswell, "A man cannot with propriety speak of himself, except he relates simple facts; as, 'I was at Richmond': or what depends on mensuration; as 'I am six feet high.' He is sure he has been at Richmond; he is sure he is six feet high; but he cannot be sure he is wise, or that he has any other excellence." In the main one assents to this ruling. And yet we are coming to see that for Religion experience is the real subject-matter with which we have immediately to deal, and every experient has value. Could we get the most backward savage to tell his actual thoughts about God we should have material for reflection of more service than a great many of our theological books. If I can shew anyone why I believe in Jesus Christ I ought to do it, and take all the risks of confessional speech.

A few years ago, at a time when there was

unusual agitation concerning the historical
character of the Christian Faith, a strong impulse arose in my mind to offer a contribution
to the discussion. I felt there was something to
be said which was generally overlooked. It
appeared to me that the claims of the ordinary
believer to a voice in the debate were not recognised to the extent the New Testament permitted. For while with us the ever-increasing
sense of the value of the trained intellect en-
courages a tendency to ignore the laic mind, in
primitive times an apostle wrote thus to all
Christian men, *Ye have an anointing from the Holy
One, and ye all know....And...the anointing which
ye received of Him abideth in you, and ye need not that
any one teach you; but as His anointing teacheth you
concerning all things...ye abide in Him.* It seemed
to me that in agreement with these words, if I,
although not a learned man, had anything to
say, I might perhaps be a voice to persons who
were in danger of depending too much upon
authority, or of suffering from the contradiction,
not of sinners, but of scholars. Accordingly,
under the title of *One Avenue to God: a Transcript
of Experience,* I published in *The Hibbert Journal*
(April 1914) an article which endeavoured to
shew the credibility of the Incarnation for minds

which cherished both individual prerogative and
the community of holy things. Now, after the
lapse of ten years I find myself viewing the
matter with an increased sense of the need to
make every man autonomous in the things of
Faith. For still the Church is suffering from
the contradiction of scholars. Books which be-
little our Lord—their authors would say that
they actualise Jesus to us—are published every
year by avowed Christians of unquestionable
learning, while, on the other side, the conserva-
tive school has its able output in defence of the
Incarnation as an historic fact. In the absence
of any overwhelming consensus of judgment
concerning the origins of Christianity, what is
the ordinary, educated layman to believe? How
is he to judge between the articles dealing with
Christ and the Gospels in the *Encyclopaedia
Biblica* and Hastings' *Dictionary of the Bible*? How
is he to listen to both the Bishop of Gloucester
and Professor Kirsopp Lake? And will the
debate between the two schools ever end?

That I do not exaggerate the uncertainties of
the position may be seen from the following
sentences: "Once we have laid stress upon
historical events as vital to our position, we
cannot warn the critic off. Where history is, the

critic has the right to come....Such an enquiry has obvious risks. If it be free, and any other type of investigation is worthless, then it must have an open mind with reference to its possible results. The chance of unfavourable decision must inevitably be taken[1]." Now Professor Peake, whose words these are, has taken those risks for himself, and has emerged from his investigations with a sure faith in the general facts and broad features of the Gospel narratives. But Professor Peake is an accomplished scholar, who has given his life to researches for which he is naturally fitted. How many ordinarily educated people have either the opportunity or the ability for such impartial and meticulous studies? For my own part, if I could do what Dr Peake and other scholars like him have done (and profoundly do I revere their conscientious and laborious work) I should still have to ask, What is to happen to my soul while my researches are proceeding? The bigger question remains, How are we, God's common people, knowing as we do of the existence of this relentless critical controversy over the Gospels, to answer the question which is so intimately bound up with the interests of our moral being, What is the

[1] *Christianity: its Nature and its Truth*, pp. 140-1.

truth about Jesus Christ? Must we go back to Rome, or shall we wash our hands of the whole business and say, as multitudes are saying to-day, We cannot tell?

One of the greatest teachers of antiquity, the Jewish Philo, in a very beautiful passage declares that there are two ways by which men may endeavour to know God. First, one may seek Him in and through those works of Nature which are His shadow. But there is also, he says, a more perfect and more highly purified kind of perception "which comprehends God through Himself." The latter way enables a man also to understand the works of God, so that he may understand this universal world[1]. In a similar strain Plotinus declares, "The perception of the highest God is not effected by science, nor by intelligence, like other intelligibles, but by the Presence of Him, which is a mode of knowledge superior to that of Science[2]." And both Philo and Plotinus point us back to the symbolic myths of Plato.

Now this hope of a comprehension of God through Himself is the method of perception clearly prescribed in the New Testament. When

[1] *Allegories of the Sacred Laws*, III. 33.
[2] *On the Good or the One*, § IV.

S. Peter made his famous confession of faith in Jesus and obtained the blessing of a new name, symbolising a new birth begun in him then, our Lord expressly attributed the confession, not to any human authority, neither to Rabbi, nor to priest, nor to Scripture, but to God's immediate action in his soul. *Flesh and blood hath not revealed it unto thee, but my Father which is in heaven.* Similarly, in the Fourth Gospel, Jesus declares, *It is written in the prophets, And they shall all be taught of God. Every one that hath heard from the Father, and hath learned, cometh unto me.* S. Paul sums up these declarations by affirming, *No man can say, Jesus is Lord, but in the Holy Spirit.*

Such sayings are based upon that self-evidencing quality of Truth which is independent alike of priest and scholar, and they justify us in the practice of patience while controversies proceed, knowing that we may answer the essential questions about Jesus Christ without tarrying for any one. It is of course true that we should not know of Him at all had not some one testified concerning Him. We are not isolated units but persons of particular places in the great family of Mankind; and we are indebted to the many hands that have combined to produce the New Testament. But to judge the truth of the New

Testament lies within the competence of every one who hears the marvellous story of Christ.

Now in order to achieve this judgment the first thing to be done is to see the Man Jesus depicted in the Gospels as they stand, without troubling ourselves at all for the moment with the question how these Gospels came to be.

To see the Man Jesus—but there are those who tell us this is impossible unless in mere fugitive glimpses. Professor Burkitt doubts whether our Gospels contain stories from 40 separate days of our Lord's life, "so that nine tenths of the public life of Jesus remains to us a blank, even if we take every recorded incident as historical and accurately reported," and all His words could be read over aloud with due gravity in six hours (*The Gospel History and its Transmission*, p. 20). And what of the unrecorded years?

But is it necessary to know more in order to see Him? There are some living men within my acquaintance whom I have certainly not seen 40 separate times, or anything like it, but about whose characters I am prepared to make quite positive affirmations. There are moments in Life when in a single deed a man reveals himself more fully than in all his previous acts. Half an hour's conversation will often unfold all the personality that is ever likely to be disclosed in mortal life. And I certainly do not think we need treat our Lord after the manner of a police ticket-of-leave. It is not much to trust Him for the unrecorded days when the recorded are what they are.

The most impressive feature of the Jesus of the Gospels to me is His ethical self-sufficiency in the face of both the requirements He makes of all others and His insistence upon our over-whelming sin-indebtedness to God (S. Matthew xviii. 21–35). Nowhere does He betray the faintest consciousness of any need of His own to offer the prayer, *Forgive us our debts as we also have forgiven our debtors.* Sin always leaves its scars—but the skin of Jesus is whole. He moves through Life as being the only quite integrate man of History.

And then, next, I should be blind not to see His matchless benevolence, and this not simply in so many isolated deeds of healing, but in His devotion, for the sake of all men, to religious ideals of the highest spirituality and the widest reach. It is to Him we owe the fundamental conception of modern international movements, the ideal of Racial Salvation. Of the scope of His work as the Sower of Truth-Seed He once observed, *The field is the World.*

And then, last, I should be deaf if I did not hear the sound of His weeping over the City of bigots that slew Him, nor the tender tones of so many of His sayings to the lost and the miserable.

These are but few and inadequate words wherewith to express outlines even of the Portrait of Jesus which the Four Gospels combined delineate. I sum them up in one word. He is *holy*, in the full New Testament sense of the term: He has the coincidence of an unfaltering will with an ethically perfect mind—perfect, that is, in correspondence with all the occasions in which His life was actually wrought out.

Now, seeing Him thus, the question of questions which I have then to ask is not, Are these things reported of Him historically true, but, Are they eternally true? That is, *Do I believe that the Creator is as Jesus was?* It does not affect that question, in the first place, that some men may dispute the correctness of the narrative as history. *Is God like that? Bishop Bloughram's Apology* puts the very point at issue,

"What think ye of Christ" friend? When all's
    done and said,
Like you this Christianity or not?
It may be false, but will you wish it true?
Has it your vote to be so if it can?

Here is a question I can answer without troubling about the disputes of scholars. My answer to it will be regulated by the extent of my confidence in the vitality of Goodness, and this will depend in turn upon the measure in which I myself am good or evil, not in positive accomplishment but in vital desire and effort. The just man believes that justice finally prevails because he feels in himself its moving spirit and authoritative verdicts. And if there be a man in whose tortuous life cunning and selfishness are entirely dominant, that man, if he thinks of God at all, will be tempted to fancy that God is altogether such an one as himself. Our working and actual creed is framed, not according to dialectic skill, but according to the stir and quality of moral instinct resident in our spirit.

Now, for my own part, when I first reached this point of view, I was like Bunyan's Christian at the Cross. A burden of distress I had long been carrying slipped from me and rolled into Christ's empty tomb. No words could fully express the relief to my spirit. For there was only one answer possible to the question thus presented to me. My whole being passionately acclaimed Jesus as Carlyle once called Him,

"Our Divinest Symbol." None could ever conceive and formulate, whether by historical process or imaginative art, the portrait of Jesus in
the Gospels except it were given Him from
above. On the other hand, men may have
abundant learning, and yet, unless the Divine
love fill them, misconstrue the simplest documents. Indeed, whenever in our discussions
about Divine things we become bitter or cen-
sorious, or petty-minded, we have missed God
Himself. The flame of the Holy Spirit has no
smoke. The man who touches Reality is filled
with an awe that solemnises and liberalises all
his being. The Love in which our manhood was
constituted at the first recognises Love and
attests it as both the Way and the End. And all
the discrepancies men see in Nature, all their
monstrous exaggerations of Nature's terrible
acts, are nothing to the man who has once
received, through Jesus the Symbol, a vision
of the Love of God.

There is a second step to which I have advanced and through this I am able to preserve
fellowship with the Church of Christ. If, as I
know is the case, the Symbol is true, if "our
fair Father Christ" expresses the reality of God,
I can look up and pray as Jesus taught us, *Our*

Father which art in Heaven. But then, if the Creator
is Fatherly, may I not work back from the
Fatherhood of God to the historic fact of
Incarnation, as necessitated by the character
of God so described? Let me illustrate the point
from literature. In more than one of his poems
Horace pays a beautiful tribute to his father as
"the best of fathers"; he relates how his father
used to go with him to his classes, and sit with
him while he was under tuition, advising him
in all the company he kept, looking at the boy's
life from the boy's side[1]. So the highest thing
man can ever think of God, and therefore the
truest thing, is that which sums up all revelation
in the watchword, *Immanuel, God with us.* Surely
it was Fatherly for God to come into the whole
of man's life, not merely as a myth into his
fancy, nor merely as a literature into the many
departments of his mind, but actually as a
Person into his manhood, which is flesh as well
as Spirit. And, if He came thus, would it not
be in some form fuller than that of an imperfect
prophet-saint? Would He have been perfect
Father if He had not crowned all past and
partial revelations by as great a gift of Himself
as simple souls could accept? For perfect Love

[1] *Satires* (*Lib.* I. vi. 81–2; cf. iv. 103–29).

must needs be a self-gift as complete as the recipient can welcome. Hence to deny the Incarnation both imperils the doctrine of the Fatherhood and belittles the capacity of man. Incarnation is Fatherhood's complete and expressive sympathy, the chosen and necessary mode—forgive the paradox—of the approach of Perfect Life to that which is faulty and unfinished.

But next the question arises, How can the Incarnation be reconciled with earthly life, how shall it be seen in its setting?

Looking back over the history of our race prior to the birth of Christ, I am reminded of the striking apothegm of a modern scholar[1]: "The main religious history, not only of Semitic but also of Aryan races, converges to Christ, and radiates again from Him." And surely no wise apprehension of the Incarnation will neglect to relate it to both past and future. For all human life must ever have had some participation in the Divine Life, reaching up to and

[1] The late Dr Bennett in *Faith and Criticism*, p. 43. I should like to pay a tribute to this eminent Hebraist, my own teacher in College days, and one who since those times has repeatedly helped me in correspondence upon matters in which he was a great authority. He set one a splendid example of sane and painstaking criticism.

overshadowed and nourished by that all-encompassing Presence in Whom every man lives and moves and has his being. Such a view would seem to be the outlook of those apostolic writers to whom we owe the Prologue to the Fourth Gospel and the Epistles to the Ephesians and to the Colossians. But the connecting thought I am seeking is found outside the New Testament in a lost Gospel, fragments of which occur in early writers, *The Gospel according to the Hebrews*. In its story of the Baptism of Jesus, we read: "It came to pass, when the Lord was come up out of the water, that the whole fountain of the Holy Spirit came down and rested on Him and said unto Him, My Son, in all the prophets I awaited Thy coming that I might rest on Thee. For Thou art my rest; Thou art My firstborn Son, who reignest for ever."

In all the prophets the Spirit of God was partially incarnate. In all He was seeking a full entrance, an Incarnation such as at last was achieved at Bethlehem. Thus a long golden beam streams through the pre-Christian ages, waxing more and more until it becomes in Jesus *the effulgence of God's Glory*. The Incarnation is the very blossom and fruitage of God's Immanence. Of the joy of those Hebrew Saints,

such as Simeon and Anna, who were permitted
to see the Lord's Christ, we may say in the
language of a Messianic prophecy, *They joy
before Thee according to the joy in harvest.* The
Bethlehem Manger was God's garner. Indeed,
the fulness of Nature was gathered in then.

> No sudden thing of glory and fear
> Was the Lord's coming; but the dear
> Slow Nature's days followed each other
> To form the Saviour from His Mother
> —One of the Children of the year.
>
> The earth, the rain, received the trust
> —The sun and dews, to frame the Just.
> He drew His daily life from these,
> According to His own decrees
> Who makes man from the fertile dust.
>
> Sweet summer and the winter wild,
> These brought Him forth, the Undefiled.
> The happy Springs renewed again
> His daily bread, the growing grain,
> The food and raiment of the Child[1].

I have come thus through the supreme idea
of the central Figure in the Gospels, apprehended
independently of criticism, to an *à priori* faith
in the Incarnation as God's historical act of
sympathy and judgment in Human Life. Behind

[1] *Advent Meditation*, Alice Meynell.

it all is Love that burns and glorifies. I do not say, as a modern sings,

That men could imagine such love is the same
To me as a living of yesterday.

Certainly I hold to the worth of such an imagination. But I see the force of an event. Whatever spiritual thing comes to expression, whether in our individual lives or in history, is more than it could be immaterialised. Things that can happen are more than things that cannot. Just because the idea of the Divine Love is so tremendously real, it is something for which Incarnation is the only adequate vehicle of expression. No one can believe in the Love of God as fully as he who cries with S. Thomas at the feet of Jesus, *My Lord and my God*.

And what once happened, crowning long ages of advent, remains. The Life which was made flesh, enhanced by the very fact of expression, has been taken back into the spiritual atmosphere of the world, to breathe Itself through our moments of openness into human lives, thus helping us to be that which It was and is. He passed beyond Death into the central tides that sweep through all beings susceptible of God. He is vaster than our dreams. All His

names fall short of our consciousness of Him
when our hearts are pure and zealous and
believing. *Thou hast magnified Thy word above all
Thy Name.* Immeasurable breadths and depths
of Life lie behind the Keeper of my soul. I can
only pray with George MacDonald,

Not in my fancy now I search to find thee;
Not in its loftiest forms would shape or bind thee.
I cry to One whom I can never know,
Filling me with an infinite overflow;
Not to a shape that dwells within my heart,
Clothed in perfections love and truth assigned
    thee,
But to the God thou knowest that thou art.

For EU product safety concerns, contact us at Calle de José Abascal, 56–1°,
28003 Madrid, Spain or eugpsr@cambridge.org.

www.ingramcontent.com/pod-product-compliance
Ingram Content Group UK Ltd.
Pitfield, Milton Keynes, MK11 3LW, UK
UKHW020315140625
459647UK00018B/1888